THE DOUBLE DIAMOND DAILY DEVOTIONAL

MIKE MURDOCK

*"Wisdom is the principal thing; therefore get wisdom:
and with all thy getting get understanding. Exalt her,
and she shall promote thee: she shall bring thee to
honour, when thou dost embrace her."*
Proverbs 4:7-8

Unless otherwise indicated, all Scripture quotations are taken from the King James Version of the Bible.

Double Diamond Daily Devotional
Copyright © 1996 by *MIKE MURDOCK*
ISBN 1-56394-052-3
All publishing rights belong exclusively to Wisdom International

Published by The Wisdom Center · P. O. Box 99 • Denton, Texas 76202
1-888-WISDOM-1 (1-888-947-3661) · Website: www.thewisdomcenter.cc

YOU CAN CREATE ANY FUTURE YOU WANT.

❑ You will never leave *where you are*, until you decide where *you would rather be.*

❑ The day you make a decision about your life is the day your world will *change.*

❑ Move *decisively* toward the goals you have established.

❑ Intolerance of your *present* creates your *future.*

WISDOM WORDS

"Remember ye not the former things, neither consider the things of old. Behold, I will do a new thing; now it shall spring forth; shall ye not know it? I will even make a way in the wilderness, and rivers in the desert."

Isaiah 43:18-19

CREATE A DAILY AGENDA.

❏ Your daily agenda is a written list of things you want to accomplish in the next 24 hours.

❏ On your written, daily "agenda"...decide your *priorities* in the order of their importance.

❏ You will never unlock your potential until your priorities become habitual.

❏ When you focus on your priorities you will eliminate confusion.

WISDOM WORDS

"Brethren, I count not myself to have apprehended: but this one thing I do, forgetting those things which are behind, and reaching forth unto those things which are before, I press toward the mark for the prize of the high calling of God in Christ Jesus."

Philippians 3:13-14

DOCUMENT YOUR GOALS.

- ❏ Take the time to write down carefully what you want to accomplish with your life.

- ❏ Writing down your goals makes you more decisive.

- ❏ The fifteen minutes you invest in making a daily schedule will be multiplied 100-fold before the end of the month.

- ❏ Visualizing your dreams and goals has power.

- ❏ Planners can predict their success.

- ❏ The secret of an achiever is his written daily schedule.

WISDOM WORDS

"And the Lord answered me, and said, Write the vision, and make it plain upon tables, that he may run that readeth it."   Habakkuk 2:2

DON'T OVER-SCHEDULE YOURSELF TODAY.

❏ The wise refuse to consider too many goals.

❏ Only write down the number of things you know you will actually complete.

❏ When you over-schedule, your attention will focus on those things you failed to accomplish instead of the tasks that have been completed.

❏ Make time only for that which is worthwhile.

WISDOM WORDS

"Be still, and know that I am God: I will be exalted among the heathen, I will be exalted in the earth."

Psalm 46:10

SET REASONABLE DEADLINES.

❏ Give yourself enough time to achieve your goal.

❏ Good things take effort and time.

❏ Be honest with yourself concerning your talent, time and resources.

❏ Focus only on those tasks that you feel worthy of your total attention and time.

WISDOM WORDS

"To every thing there is a season, and a time to every purpose under the heaven:"   Ecclesiastes 3:1

RESPECT YOUR DREAMS AND GOALS.

❑ What you respect, you will attract.

❑ Respect is needed for excitement.

❑ Excitement is needed for your energy.

❑ Energy is needed for completion of your dreams and goals.

WISDOM WORDS

"And also that every man should eat and drink, and enjoy the good of all his labour, it is the gift of God."
Ecclesiastes 3:13

FOCUS! FOCUS! FOCUS!

❑ Focus on one task at a time.

❑ Abandon yourself totally to each hour.

❑ Remember that satan's greatest goal is "broken focus."

❑ Focus creates momentum.

— *WISDOM WORDS* —

"Only be thou strong and very courageous, that thou mayest observe to do according to all the law, which Moses My servant commanded thee: turn not from it to the right hand or to the left, that thou mayest prosper whithersoever thou goest."   Joshua 1:7

TALK ABOUT YOUR EXCITEMENT.

❑ Enthusiasm breeds excitement.

❑ Your energy will attract others to your dream.

❑ Thought and talk magnify anything.

❑ Enthusiasm is the only climate the Seeds of Success will grow.

❑ If you want others to get involved in your dreams and goals you must exude an aura of excitement.

WISDOM WORDS

"Death and life are in the power of the tongue: and they that love it shall eat the fruit thereof."

Proverbs 18:21

MASTER THE ENEMY OF FATIGUE.

❑ Fatigue is the number one enemy of your progress and joy.

❑ When fatigue walks in, faith walks out.

❑ You can achieve more in one hour if you are rested than you can accomplish in eight hours if your body is weary and worn out.

❑ Rest your body —good health is life's first prize.

WISDOM WORDS

"And He said unto them, Come ye yourselves apart into a desert place, and rest a while: for there were many coming and going, and they had no leisure so much as to eat."   Mark 6:31

DRESS APPROPRIATELY.

- ❏ Your clothing communicates an attitude toward the goals you are pursuing.

- ❏ People *see* what you are before they *hear* what you are.

- ❏ *You are a walking message system to others.*

- ❏ Even Joseph dressed to create acceptance in the palace of Pharaoh.

WISDOM WORDS

"Then Pharaoh sent and called Joseph, and they brought him hastily out of the dungeon: and he shaved himself, and changed his raiment, and came in unto Pharaoh."

Genesis 41:14

TREASURE YOUR MENTOR.

- ❑ Your mentor is anyone who consistently teaches you what you want to know.

- ❑ It was the secret of Elijah and Elisha; Moses and Joshua; Paul and Timothy.

- ❑ Mentorship is accepting perfect knowledge from an imperfect man.

- ❑ Pursue and extract the knowledge of the mentors that God has made available to your life.

- ❑ You will never travel beyond your Wisdom.

WISDOM WORDS

"A wise man will hear, and will increase learning; and a man of understanding shall attain unto wise counsels:"
Proverbs 1:5

ASK OTHERS TO BE A PART OF YOUR GOAL.

❑ God never intended for you to succeed alone.

❑ What you lack is always housed in someone else.

❑ When you pray today, ask God to direct you to someone He has chosen to make a contribution to your life.

WISDOM WORDS

"Ask, and it shall be given you; seek, and ye shall find; knock, and it shall be opened unto you:"

Matthew 7:7

DISCOVER YOUR DREAM.

- ❑ Every dream is born or borrowed.

- ❑ It is born within your own heart or subconsciously borrowed from someone who has influenced you.

- ❑ Whatever creates joy and energy within you is probably an indication of what God wants you to pursue.

- ❑ Your dominant talent is the center of your expertise. Your success is *there*.

WISDOM WORDS

"And unto one He gave five talents, to another two, and to another one; to every man according to his several ability; and straightway took His journey."

Matthew 25:15

PROTECT YOUR DREAM-SEED.

- ❏ God hangs photographs in your heart, of something you can become…do…or have.

- ❏ A Dream-Seed is the invisible photograph of a desired miracle, goal or dream.

- ❏ Abraham nurtured that inner picture of many generations of children through his promised son, Isaac.

- ❏ Guard, with all diligence, that Dream-Seed that God has planted in your heart, through prayer and discretion.

WISDOM WORDS

"Finally, brethren, whatsoever things are true, whatsoever things are honest, whatsoever things are just, whatsoever things are pure, whatsoever things are lovely, whatsoever things are of good report; if there be any virtue, and if there be any praise, think on these things."   Philippians 4:8

MAKE GOD YOUR DREAM-PARTNER.

- ❑ A God-inspired dream will always require the participation of God.

- ❑ One hour with God could easily reveal to you the fatal flaws in your most carefully laid plans.

- ❑ He who succeeds in prayer…succeeds.

- ❑ Let God decide your daily agenda…and your dream will be achieved.

WISDOM WORDS

"Not that we are sufficient of ourselves to think any thing as of ourselves; but our sufficiency is of God;"

2 Corinthians 3:5

DON'T PURSUE YESTERDAY'S DREAM.

❑ What excites you in your youth may bore you when you are older.

❑ Be willing to relinquish previous goals that no longer stimulate you.

❑ Don't be a prisoner to your dreams of earlier years.

❑ You are not a loser just because you do not finish something you no longer desire.

WISDOM WORDS

"Remember ye not the former things, neither consider the things of old."   Isaiah 43:18

FIGHT FOR YOUR DREAM.

- ❑ Don't let others distract you from God's Assignment for your life.

- ❑ Avoid over-scheduling today to accommodate the expectations of others.

- ❑ Don't feel obligated to relationships that demotivate you.

WISDOM WORDS

"Blessed be the Lord my strength, which teacheth my hands to war, and my fingers to fight:"

Psalm 144:1

CELEBRATE THOSE WHO LOVE YOUR GOALS.

❑ Recognize those God sends into your life to inspire and energize you.

❑ Acknowledge helpful insights gladly, and resist the temptation to become defensive and belligerent.

❑ Find ways to reward those who have made your goals and dreams come true.

WISDOM WORDS

"He that walketh with wise men shall be wise: but a companion of fools shall be destroyed."

Proverbs 13:20

REFUSE TO QUIT.

❑ The secret of champions is their refusal to quit trying.

❑ Futility is merely a feeling…conquer it and keep heading toward your goals.

❑ Create small successes when the large ones seem impossible.

❑ Even skyscrapers are built a brick at a time.

WISDOM WORDS

"For precept must be upon precept, precept upon precept; line upon line, line upon line; here a little, and there a little:" Isaiah 28:10

SOW A PART
OF YOURSELF
EVERY DAY.

❑ A Seed is anything you can do that benefits another person.

❑ Your respect for others is a Seed...sow it.

❑ Your knowledge given to others is a Seed...sow it.

❑ What you make happen for others, God will make happen for you.

WISDOM WORDS

"Knowing that whatsoever good thing any man doeth, the same shall he receive of the Lord, whether he be bond or free."   Ephesians 6:8

BE WILLING TO SOMETIMES DREAM ALONE.

❑ Every champion must be willing to believe in his own dream when others seem too busy or uncaring to encourage him.

❑ Every great inventor, such as Thomas Edison, faced waves of ridicule and scorn before their genius was recognized and appreciated.

❑ Don't forget to keep your focus on where you are going and refuse to be discouraged by the present circumstances that will soon pass.

WISDOM WORDS

"I will never leave thee, nor forsake thee."

Hebrews 13:5

RE-EVALUATE YOUR CURRENT GOALS.

❑ Never hesitate to reappraise your goals and what you really want to accomplish.

❑ Remember that your goals are birthed out of needs… and your needs are often seasonal.

❑ Celebrate every page of progress toward your goals.

❑ Don't keep pursuing a dream no longer capable of energizing you.

WISDOM WORDS

"For which of you, intending to build a tower, sitteth not down first, and counteth the cost, whether he have sufficient to finish it?"   Luke 14:28

CHOOSE A PROVEN MENTOR.

- ❏ Those you admire, eternally effect your future.

- ❏ Choose a mentor who increases your faith in God.

- ❏ Learn from the scars of your mentor as well as his sermons.

WISDOM WORDS

"And we beseech you, brethren, to know them which labour among you, and are over you in the Lord, and admonish you; And to esteem them very highly in love for their work's sake."   1 Thessalonians 5:12-13

DEFINE THE TRUE CONTRIBUTION OF EVERY FRIENDSHIP.

❑ Each person in your life is a current…taking you toward your goals or away from them.

❑ Do not expect a 3 x 5 friendship to grow your 16 x 20 dream.

❑ The worth of any friendship can be measured by its contribution to God's Assignment to your life.

❑ He who does not increase you inevitably will decrease you.

WISDOM WORDS

"Be not deceived: evil communications corrupt good manners." 1 Corinthians 15:33

ACCEPT OPPOSITION AS PROOF OF YOUR PROGRESS.

- ❑ Warfare always surrounds the birth of a miracle.

- ❑ Nothing is ever as bad as it first appears.

- ❑ Battle is the opportunity to prove what you believe.

- ❑ Joseph proved that opposition is the wave that takes you from the pit to the palace.

WISDOM WORDS

"In God have I put my trust: I will not be afraid what man can do unto me."   Psalm 56:11

EXPECT YOUR SEED OF PATIENCE TO PRODUCE A HARVEST.

❑ Every dreamer must tolerate seasons of waiting.

❑ Waiting is not wasted time.

❑ Moses proved that leaders are not trained in the palace, but in the desert.

❑ Each day of waiting is proof of your trust in God.

WISDOM WORDS

"The Lord is good unto them that wait for Him, to the soul that seeketh Him."   Lamentations 3:25

"But they that wait upon the Lord shall renew their strength; they shall mount up with wings as eagles; they shall run, and not be weary; and they shall walk, and not faint."   Isaiah 40:31

INSIST ON TODAY'S PRODUCTIVITY.

❏ An unproductive day is an unhappy day.

❏ You were created to be productive…to accomplish… to multiply.

❏ Any progress toward your life dream today should be celebrated.

❏ Each hour is an "employee"…give it a specific Assignment.

WISDOM WORDS

"And God blessed them, and God said unto them, Be fruitful, and multiply, and replenish the earth, and subdue it: and have dominion over the fish of the sea, and over the fowl of the air, and over every living thing that moveth upon the earth." Genesis 1:28

TAKE A TINY STEP TODAY TOWARD YOUR LIFETIME GOAL.

❏ Champions are those who are willing to move forward an inch at a time.

❏ Stay in movement today.

❏ Break down your goal into many small steps.

❏ Progress creates joy.

WISDOM WORDS

"For who hath despised the day of small things?"
Zechariah 4:10

GET MOVING TOWARD GOD'S ASSIGNMENT FOR YOUR LIFE.

❑ You will never possess what you are unwilling to pursue.

❑ Race horses never win races while they are in stalls.

❑ God rewards reachers.

❑ Your enthusiasm will attract the right people in your life.

WISDOM WORDS

"The steps of a good man are ordered by the Lord: and He delighteth in his way."   Psalm 37:23

GIVE EACH HOUR AN ASSIGNMENT.

- ❏ Your life is like a train on the Track of Success.

- ❏ Each day God gives you 24 golden box cars (hours) to load up.

- ❏ What you place in each box car, or hour, determines the speed and the distance your train will move toward your next city of accomplishment.

- ❏ Make your life count today.

WISDOM WORDS

"Redeeming the time, because the days are evil."
Ephesians 5:16

CELEBRATE WISDOM TODAY.

❏ Wisdom is doing what God would do in your present circumstance.

❏ Wisdom comes from the Word of God.

❏ Solomon said that Wisdom is the Miracle Key that unlocks life's house of treasures.

❏ Wisdom requires effort, time and persistence but is worth the cost.

WISDOM WORDS

"Wisdom is the principal thing; therefore get wisdom: and with all thy getting get understanding. Exalt her, and she shall promote thee: she shall bring thee to honour, when thou dost embrace her."

Proverbs 4:7,8

SEND SOMEONE A SIGNAL THAT THEY MATTER.

❑ Everyone needs reassurance of their worth.

❑ Remind yourself throughout today that each person you meet has encountered waves of criticism, condemnation and inferiority... you can change this.

❑ Your words of reassurance can be like water on their Seeds of Hope.

WISDOM WORDS

"The Lord God hath given me the tongue of the learned, that I should know how to speak a word in season to him that is weary:"   Isaiah 50:4

ABANDON ABUSIVE FRIENDSHIPS.

❑ There are four kinds of people in your life: those who add, subtract, divide and multiply.

❑ Those who do not increase you, inevitably will decrease you.

❑ It is the responsibility of others to discern your worth.

── *WISDOM WORDS* ──

"Make no friendship with an angry man; and with a furious man thou shalt not go: Lest thou learn his ways, and get a snare to thy soul."　　Proverbs 22:24-25

COMPLIMENT SOMEONE TODAY.

❑ A popular, but inaccurate statement is, "words are cheap." Nothing could be farther from the truth.

❑ Words *cause* wars. Words *settle* wars. Words *create* the waves of emotion that control our world.

❑ Your words of kindness today could easily create the wave that carries someone to their dream.

── *WISDOM WORDS* ──

"Death and life are in the power of the tongue: and they that love it shall eat the fruit thereof."

Proverbs 18:21

CONFIDE IN FEW.

- ❑ Someone has said that even a fish wouldn't get caught if it kept its mouth *shut!*

- ❑ Confidence is a *gift* to be shared in the privacy of prayer or with an intercessor God has assigned to your life.

- ❑ Never share your troubles with someone *unqualified* to help you.

WISDOM WORDS

"...discover not a secret to another: Lest he that heareth it put thee to shame, and thine infamy turn not away."
Proverbs 25:9-10

SHOWCASE ANOTHER'S OPINION.

❑ One of the greatest gifts you will ever give anyone is…the Gift of Recognition.

❑ Every husband…wife…and child…is authorized by the Creator to have a viewpoint, and an opportunity to express it.

❑ Honor their right to be heard.

WISDOM WORDS

"Let nothing be done through strife or vainglory; but in lowliness of mind let each esteem other better than themselves." Philippians 2:3

QUENCH THE URGE TO JUDGE.

☐ You cannot draw conclusions as long as there is missing information.

☐ Things are never as they first appear. Reserve judgment.

☐ Never attempt to explain…or penalize someone for actions you do not fully understand.

─ *WISDOM WORDS* ─

"Therefore thou art inexcusable, O man, whosoever thou art that judgest: for wherein thou judgest another, thou condemnest thyself; for thou that judgest doest the same things."   Romans 2:1

MAKE SMILE YOUR STYLE.

___

❏ Your face *telegraphs* your attitude…toward *life*… toward *others*…about *yourself.*

❏ Your countenance *creates a climate that attracts* people toward you or causes them to move away from you.

❏ When you smile *first,* you have decided the direction the relationship will go.

WISDOM WORDS

"Who is as the wise man? and who knoweth the interpretation of a thing? a man's wisdom maketh his face to shine, and the boldness of his face shall be changed."   Ecclesiastes 8:1

DEVELOP THE GIFT OF ROMANCE.

- ❏ Romance is when you deliberately *create a special moment* or *memorable event* in someone's life.

- ❏ Don't wait for your mate to create a perfect occasion.

- ❏ Aggressively, creatively and with spontaneity start scheduling unique moments and methods to express your love.

- ❏ To be unforgotten, do something *unforgettable today*.

WISDOM WORDS

"For this cause shall a man leave his father and mother, and shall be joined unto his wife, and they two shall be one flesh."   Ephesians 5:31

LEARN SOMETHING "NEW" ABOUT SOMEONE YOU LOVE.

❑ *Knowledge increases confidence.* The more knowledgeable you become about someone, the more capable you become at anticipating their needs.

❑ Develop a Personal Portfolio of their particular preferences, such as favorite car, food, colors, songs, books and secret ambitions.

❑ Our Heavenly Father created uniqueness to be discovered, appreciated and *celebrated*.

❑ Greatness will unfold with each discovery.

WISDOM WORDS

"And the Lord make you to increase and abound in love one toward another,"   1 Thessalonians 3:12

INTERVIEW YOUR CHILDREN.

- ❏ Your child is worth knowing. *Really* knowing.

- ❏ Talk. Exchange. Observe. Carefully collect any piece of information that paints a portrait of this "heritage of the Lord."

- ❏ Communicate with the intent to *learn*, not condemn.

- ❏ Give your child what he cannot find anywhere else —*non-judgmental conversation*—and he will keep coming back.

WISDOM WORDS

"Lo, children are an heritage of the Lord: and the fruit of the womb is his reward. As arrows are in the hand of a mighty man; so are children of the youth. Happy is the man that hath his quiver full of them: they shall not be ashamed, but they shall speak with the enemies in the gate." Psalm 127:3-5

GENERATE ENERGY.

❏ God *energizes*. In Genesis 1, He created...moved...
spoke...divided...called...and so forth.

❏ You are His offering. *You were created for movement.*
Your tongue speaks. Your eyes see. Your ears hear.
Your hands grasp. Your feet walk. Even your mind
creates thoughts, *each containing a different measure
of energy*.

❏ You are a Living Current, carrying others into your
future. Use your life today to excite others about
the God you serve and *the future made possible*
through a commitment to Jesus Christ.

WISDOM WORDS
"For in Him we live, and move, and have our being;"
Acts 17:28

INTERROGATE YOUR FRIENDS.

❑ Everyone is a Well of Information. *Draw from it.* Drop your bucket regularly into that Well.

❑ Schedule an appointment this week with your three most successful friends.

❑ Bring your list of most important questions and *get the answers you need.*

FURNISH GENTLENESS.

❏ Gentleness is like heat in a cold world.

❏ Those around you bear the wounds of Rivalry, Jealousy and Inferiority.

❏ *Pour the Oil of Gentleness* and you will become their greatest memory of the day.

WISDOM WORDS

"And the servant of the Lord must not strive; but be gentle unto all men, apt to teach, patient,"
2 Timothy 2:24

SOW AFFECTION GENEROUSLY.

- ❑ Hospital tests have proven that even babies will die if they do not receive touching and loving affection.

- ❑ *You are not an exception.*

- ❑ Reach out to someone today. *Touch...hug.*

WISDOM WORDS

"Be kindly affectioned one to another with brotherly love; in honour preferring one another;"

Romans 12:10

INSIST ON INTEGRITY.

❑ Integrity is *truthfulness*. It is doing what you say you will do.

❑ *Demand* it from yourself and *reward* it in others.

❑ Do right by others and God will do right by you.

WISDOM WORDS

"Judge me, O Lord; for I have walked in mine integrity: I have trusted also in the Lord; therefore I shall not slide."   Psalm 26:1

"Better is the poor that walketh in his integrity, than he that is perverse in his lips, and is a fool."
                                                           Proverbs 19:1

REPROVE WITH SENSITIVITY.

- ❏ *Criticism hurts.* Even when you give it in love.

- ❏ Yet, it is your personal responsibility to provide caution, correction and warnings when someone you love is on the brink of disaster.

- ❏ Your instruction is their opportunity for *promotion* from God.

WISDOM WORDS

"Poverty and shame shall be to him that refuseth instruction: but he that regardeth reproof shall be honoured."   Proverbs 13:18

CELEBRATE THOSE WHO CELEBRATE YOU.

❑ Those who discern your worth deserve special recognition.

❑ Even Jesus instructed His disciples to respect those who received them and disconnect from those who rejected them.

❑ *Go where your contribution is celebrated.* Jesus did.

WISDOM WORDS

"And into whatsoever city or town ye shall enter, inquire who in it is worthy; and there abide till ye go thence. And when ye come into an house, salute it. And if the house be worthy, let your peace come upon it: but if it be not worthy, let your peace return to you."

Matthew 10:11-13

TALK IT OUT.

- ❏ Friendships die through *neglect*.

- ❏ Don't expect others to read your mind. *Voice your concerns* over any offense and *express your desire* to make things right.

- ❏ Silence often waters the Root of Bitterness. *Talk it out*.

WISDOM WORDS

"Moreover if thy brother shall trespass against thee, go and tell him his fault between thee and him alone: if he shall hear thee, thou hast gained thy brother."

Matthew 18:15

RESURRECT HOPE IN SOMEONE TODAY.

❑ Hope is the expectation of *favorable changes.*

❑ Don't permit someone you love to remain depressed and devastated by their present circumstances.

❑ Remind them that Jesus Christ is still the Healer and Miracle-Worker in *every* circumstance of life.

WISDOM WORDS

"But sanctify the Lord God in your hearts: and be ready always to give an answer to every man that asketh you a reason of the hope that is in you with meekness and fear:"   1 Peter 3:15

SKIP WARFARE TODAY.

- ❏ Make today a peaceable day.

- ❏ Don't feed an argumentative spirit in those around you.

- ❏ Insist on praying together with those who pursue points of disagreement.

- ❏ God is well-known for *honoring* peacemakers.

WISDOM WORDS

"If it be possible, as much as lieth in you, live peaceably with all men."   Romans 12:18

TRIUMPH OVER TRIVIA.

- ❑ Think of each friendship as a beautiful flower in the garden of *your* life.

- ❑ That garden must be nurtured, fertilized and watered *regularly*.

- ❑ Don't let petty and insignificant differences—Trivia —sap the beauty of those flowers.

WISDOM WORDS

"Let all bitterness, and wrath, and anger, and clamour, and evil speaking, be put away from you, with all malice: And be ye kind one to another, tenderhearted, forgiving one another, even as God for Christ's sake hath forgiven you."
                                                    Ephesians 4:31-32

SALVAGE SOMEONE.

- ❑ You are not the only person who is struggling today.

- ❑ Others around you are hurting too.

- ❑ *Be extremely attentive to the silent cries* of someone close to you who may be drowning in the Ocean of Helplessness.

- ❑ Permit God to make you their life-jacket.

WISDOM WORDS

"Brethren, if a man be overtaken in a fault, ye which are spiritual, restore such an one in the spirit of meekness; considering thyself, lest thou also be tempted."   Galatians 6:1

NEVER COMPLAIN ABOUT WHAT YOU PERMIT.

❑ Your circumstances are not permanent.

❑ You have permitted your present circumstances or they would not exist.

❑ What you tolerate, you authorize to exist.

❑ Either accept the present without complaint or make a decision to *use your faith* and *attract a miracle* from God.

WISDOM WORDS

"Jesus said unto him, If thou canst believe, all things are possible to him that believeth."   Mark 9:23

FRIENDSHIPS.

❑ Don't permit the name of a friend to be maligned in your presence.

❑ Don't absorb a slanderous report about a friend, unless he is present to defend himself.

❑ A good friend is worth any *price*, any *effort*, any *defense*.

WISDOM WORDS

"A man that hath friends must shew himself friendly: and there is a friend that sticketh closer than a brother."
Proverbs 18:24

WITHDRAW FROM CONTENTIOUS PEOPLE.

- ❑ A contentious person is a trouble-maker. He spreads discontent, frustration and distrust.

- ❑ He gossips. He slanders. He promotes strife.

- ❑ Do not feed a relationship with such a person.

WISDOM WORDS

"As coals are to burning coals, and wood to fire; so is a contentious man to kindle strife."   Proverbs 26:21

KEEP YOUR WORD.

- ❑ Carefully review and fulfill any vows, promises or pledges you have made to anyone.

- ❑ *Never promise what you cannot produce.*

- ❑ Make things right with anyone you have wronged in the past.

WISDOM WORDS

"A good name is rather to be chosen than great riches, and loving favour rather than silver and gold."

Proverbs 22:1

RECOGNIZE THAT OTHERS INCREASE YOUR WORTH.

❑ Your *best* qualities will surface in the presence of good people.

❑ Treasure any friend who generates *energy* and *enthusiasm* toward your dreams or goals.

❑ Go the extra mile to nurture and protect any God-given relationship.

WISDOM WORDS

"Two are better than one; because they have a good reward for their labour. For if they fall, the one will lift up his fellow: but woe to him that is alone when he falleth; for he hath not another to help him up."

Ecclesiastes 4:9-10

MAKE ANGER WORK FOR YOU.

❑ Anger is energy. *Harness it.*

❑ Some anger can be devastating to your family, your career or your life. You can *master* it through prayer or channel it in a worthwhile project.

❑ *Direct* your anger towards your true adversary, satan, instead of those you love.

WISDOM WORDS

"Be ye angry, and sin not: let not the sun go down upon your wrath: Neither give place to the devil."

Ephesians 4:26-27

CHOOSE TO BELIEVE IN MIRACLES.

❑ You serve a God of Miracles. A miracle is the *supernatural intervention of God in the problems of your life.*

❑ By believing in the Power of God, you have nothing to lose and everything to gain.

❑ At some point in your life, you will either be forced to live in the *potential of your faith*, or with the *consequences of your doubt*.

WISDOM WORDS

"Jesus said unto him, 'If thou canst believe, all things are possible to him that believeth.'" Mark 9:23

NEVER DOUBT THE LOVE OF GOD.

❑ The World's Greatest Miracle happened 2000 years ago. God gave His Son Jesus to die on the cross for our sins. *Calvary was a miracle.*

❑ His mercy and forgiveness are *proof* that He cares. Your life, your health and your happiness *matter.*

❑ The same God who removes the *stain* of sin from your *heart*, also removes sickness, disease and poverty from your life. His *love* should make it easier for you to expect your miracle today.

WISDOM WORDS

"For God so loved the world, that He gave His only begotten Son, that whosoever believeth in Him should not perish, but have everlasting life." John 3:16

RESPECT THE LAW OF AGREEMENT.

❑ Satan fears *relationship.* He made no attempt to destroy Adam until Eve entered his life. *Two are better than one.*

❑ God celebrates *unity.* He honors *agreement* regarding your miracle.

❑ Be *quick to recognize* a God-sent prayer partner.

WISDOM WORDS

"Verily I say unto you, Whatsoever ye shall bind on earth shall be bound in heaven: and whatsoever ye shall loose on earth shall be loosed in heaven. Again I say unto you, That if two of you shall agree on earth as touching any thing that they shall ask, it shall be done for them of My Father which is in heaven."   Matthew 18:18-19

CONFESS AND FORSAKE ANY KNOWN SIN.

- ❑ *Guilt is the Thief of Faith.*

- ❑ When you permit sin in your life, you become *uncomfortable* in the presence of God.

- ❑ It is difficult to expect a miracle from a God you resent. *Confess your failure.* He forgives.

WISDOM WORDS

"If I regard iniquity in my heart, the Lord will not hear me:" Psalm 66:18

PURSUE YOUR MIRACLE.

❑ Pursuit is the *proof* of Desire. When you really want something you are willing to *reach* for it.

❑ Miracles happen *only* to those who *seek* them.

❑ The blind man *cried* out to Jesus. The hemorrhaging woman *pressed* through the crowd to touch His garment. You too, must be *willing* to put forth an *effort*. Use your Faith to get what you want from God.

— WISDOM WORDS —

"Ask, and it shall be given you; seek, and ye shall find; knock, and it shall be opened unto you: For every one that asketh receiveth; and he that seeketh findeth; and to him that knocketh it shall be opened."

Matthew 7:7-8

FOCUS YOUR FAITH.

❑ Be very *specific* when you ask God for a Miracle.

❑ Be exact in your request for a specific salary increase or business opportunity. Don't simply ask for "more" finances.

❑ Focus on the particular need you want God to meet. Don't let anyone's attitude or words distract you.

WISDOM WORDS

"Or what man is there of you, whom if his son ask bread, will he give him a stone? Or if he ask a fish, will he give him a serpent? If ye then, being evil, know how to give good gifts unto your children, how much more shall your Father which is in heaven give good things to them that ask Him?" Matthew 7:9-11

HOLD OUT FOR THE BEST.

❑ Cling to the promises of God. Don't be enticed into accepting less than God's very best for your life.

❑ Substitutions are common satanic ploys. Jesus was proof that God cared enough to send His *best*.

❑ Your faith cannot respond to two targets. So, never consider any alternative to your miracle.

WISDOM WORDS

"But let him ask in faith, nothing wavering. For he that wavereth is like a wave of the sea driven with the wind and tossed. For let not that man think that he shall receive any thing of the Lord. A double minded man is unstable in all his ways."   James 1:6-8

DISCARD YOUR DOUBTS.

❑ Miracles happen only to the *believing*. So *believe*.

❑ Doubts never produce your desired results.

❑ Stop advertising your doubts. Start *celebrating your expectations* of a miracle.

— WISDOM WORDS —

"Verily I say unto you, If ye have faith, and doubt not, ye shall not only do this which is done to the fig tree, but also if ye shall say unto this mountain, Be thou removed, and be thou cast into the sea; it shall be done."
Matthew 21:21

SPEAK TO YOUR MOUNTAIN.

❑ Your mountain is any problem that you are facing. Address it with authority and command it to move in the name of Jesus.

❑ Every mountain is a *servant* to your *faith*. It *must* obey. Few have mastered the art of verbally *commanding* their mountains to *move*.

❑ Losers talk about their mountain...Champions talk *to* their mountain.

WISDOM WORDS

"Whosoever shall say unto this mountain, Be thou removed, and be thou cast into the sea; and shall not doubt in his heart, but shall believe that those things which he saith shall come to pass; he shall have whatsoever he saith."   Mark 11:23

ACCEPT THE UNEXPLAINABLE.

❑ You can select your *miracle,* but *only God can choose the method* or means by which He sends it to you.

❑ Jesus used clay and spittle in the healing of the blind man…filling up water pots to create wine at the marriage of Cana. His methods are puzzling, unpredictable and always illogical to the natural mind of man.

❑ *Those who argue over the "methods" of God rarely receive the Miracles of God.*

─── WISDOM WORDS ───

"For My thoughts are not your thoughts, neither are your ways My ways, saith the Lord. For as the heavens are higher than the earth, so are My ways higher than your ways, and My thoughts than your thoughts."

Isaiah 55:8-9

EXPECT A TURN-AROUND.

- ❑ Today is not *permanent*. Your worst circumstances today are subject to *change*.

- ❑ God is stepping into the arena of your life. He is turning the tide in your favor.

- ❑ *You are never as far from a miracle as it first appears.*

— *WISDOM WORDS* —

"Every valley shall be exalted, and every mountain and hill shall be made low: and the crooked shall be made straight, and the rough places plain: And the glory of the Lord shall be revealed, and all flesh shall see it together: for the mouth of the Lord hath spoken it."

Isaiah 40:4-5

PRACTICE FAITH-TALK.

❑ *Your words are deciding tomorrow.*

❑ Every word you speak today will paint a portrait of faith, both in your mind and the minds of those around you.

❑ Today, season *every conversation* with *Faith-Talk*. Tell everyone what you are expecting God to do in *your* life.

WISDOM WORDS

"Finally, brethren, whatsoever things are true, whatsoever things are honest, whatsoever things are just, whatsoever things are pure, whatsoever things are lovely, whatsoever things are of good report; if there be any virtue, and if there be any praise, think on these things."   Philippians 4:8

CELEBRATE THE HEALER.

❑ Sickness comes from satan. Jesus comes to *destroy* the works of the devil.

❑ God really wants you to be well, healthy and whole. Jesus has *already paid the price* through the stripes He bore on Calvary.

❑ *Celebrate* His healing presence through you right now.

WISDOM WORDS

"How God anointed Jesus of Nazareth with the Holy Ghost and with power: Who went about doing good, and healing all that were oppressed of the devil; for God was with Him."   Acts 10:38

MAKE UP YOUR MIND TO BE HEALED.

❑ *Whatever you can tolerate, you cannot change.*

❑ *Become tenacious.* Resist sickness. Cling to the Healer.

❑ Your persistence will *demoralize* satan and *attract the attention of God.*

❑ *Demons dread a fighter.*

— *WISDOM WORDS* —

"And, behold, a woman, which was diseased with an issue of blood twelve years, came behind Him, and touched the hem of His garment: For she said within herself, If I may but touch His garment, I shall be whole."
Matthew 9:20-21

DON'T LIMIT GOD.

❏ You are the *creation*. He is your *Creator*. You cannot *out-think* the One Who made you.

❏ He delights in performing the *impossible*. He turns sickness into health...poverty into prosperity...tears into laughter.

❏ He is the Master of the Turn-around. Don't underestimate Him.

WISDOM WORDS

"With men it is impossible, but not with God: for with God all things are possible."   Mark 10:27

BIND AND RESTRAIN SATANIC ATTACKS.

❑ You are a child of God. You carry His authority on earth. *Satan is subject to you.*

❑ He must yield to the *knowledgeable* believer.

❑ Declare aloud now, "Satan, take your hands off my home, my family, my health, my finances, in Jesus' Name."

WISDOM WORDS

"Whatsoever ye shall bind on earth shall be bound in heaven: and whatsoever ye shall loose on earth shall be loosed in heaven."   Matthew 18:18

RECEIVE MINISTERS WHO TEACH MIRACLES.

❑ When men of God talk...*listen.* Ministers are *gifts* of God to the church.

❑ When God talks to the Body of Christ, He speaks through men and women.

❑ If you want your faith to grow—you must be willing to be *taught* and *mentored* by those who carry God's special anointing for healing and miracles.

WISDOM WORDS

"And He gave some, apostles; and some, prophets; and some, evangelists; and some, pastors and teachers; For the perfecting of the saints, for the work of the ministry, for the edifying of the body of Christ:"

Ephesians 4:11-12

CREATE A MIRACLE-CLIMATE.

- ❏ *Atmosphere matters.* An atmosphere of praise and worship can unlock your faith for miracles.

- ❏ When David played his harp for Saul, evil spirits *departed* from the palace. *Anointed* music is one of the master keys in creating a miracle-climate.

- ❏ Keep a cassette player handy. *Use it* to make a conscious effort today to keep Godly music playing all day long.

WISDOM WORDS

"But now bring me a minstrel. And it came to pass, when the minstrel played, that the hand of the Lord came upon him."   2 Kings 3:15

FEED YOUR FAITH DAILY.

- ❏ *Faith is your confidence in God.* Sometimes it is weak or may even seem nonexistent. At other times, it may be powerful and incredibly strong. It depends on the food you feed it.

- ❏ Faith is a *tool*…a *key*…a *weapon*. A Tool to create a future; a Key to unlock God's Storehouse of Blessing; and the Weapon that defeats satan.

- ❏ *Faith comes when you hear God talk.* Listen today to His Spirit, His Servants, His Scriptures.

WISDOM WORDS

"So then faith cometh by hearing, and hearing by the word of God."   Romans 10:17

DARE TO DREAM AGAIN.

❏ *Wake up the Dreamer within you.*

❏ Stop looking at where you have *been* and start looking at *where you are going.* Tomorrow is not here yet. *Birth it.*

❏ God is a God of the Second-Chance. He is a God of Miracles. *He has never changed His plans for your life.* Seasons change, but God's promises to you have not. *Your miracle is just ahead.*

WISDOM WORDS

"The glory of this latter house shall be greater than of the former, saith the Lord of hosts: and in this place will I give peace, saith the Lord of hosts." Haggai 2:9

PREPARE FOR MIRACLES TODAY.

❑ You have planted your Seeds. You have waited patiently for a Harvest. *It is time.*

❑ *Delay is not denial.* Like an unborn child in a mother's womb, you have been carrying the Seed of your miracle within you. Faithfully. *Expectantly.*

❑ *God always keeps His appointments.* Expect something incredible to happen *today.*

WISDOM WORDS

"For the vision is yet for an appointed time, but at the end it shall speak, and not lie: though it tarry, wait for it; because it will surely come, it will not tarry."

Habakkuk 2:3

MARCH 22
MIRACLES

HONOR A POINT-OF-CONTACT.

❏ Your point-of-contact is anything God may instruct you to do, to help you *release your faith.*

❏ The Israelites obeyed God's command to walk around the walls of Jericho. The widow of Zarephath *planted her food* as a Seed into the ministry of Elijah. *Your point-of-contact is any act of obedience that proves your faith in God.*

❏ It is unexplainable, yet powerful. So, simply do *whatever God tells you to do today.*

WISDOM WORDS

"His mother saith unto the servants, Whatsoever He saith unto you, do it."   John 2:5

EXPECT YOUR MIRACLE.

❑ Expectation is *acting as if your miracle has already happened.*

❑ Organize your life around your expected miracle. Plan it. Talk it. *Believe it.*

❑ *Expectation qualifies you for receivership.* It separates you. It transfers you from the masses who *need* miracles…to the chosen who *receive* them.

WISDOM WORDS

"But without faith it is impossible to please Him; for he that cometh to God must believe that He is, and that He is a rewarder of them that diligently seek Him."

Hebrews 11:6

DECIDE TO RECEIVE.

❑ Your Seed is *anything you plant to create a desired result or Harvest.*

❑ Your *Harvest is any benefit or blessing you have decided to receive from God.*

❑ Your *Source* is Jehovah-Jireh, the God who provides. He is unlimited, impartial and generous.

WISDOM WORDS

"But my God shall supply all your need according to His riches in glory by Christ Jesus."   Philippians 4:19

TALK TOTAL PROSPERITY.

- ❑ *You are the offspring of a perfect God. Talk like it.*

- ❑ His covenant with you is forever. *Think like it.*

- ❑ His prosperity is penetrating every area of your life. *Live like it.*

WISDOM WORDS

"Beloved, I wish above all things that thou mayest prosper and be in health, even as thy soul prospereth."
3 John 1:2

GET EXCITED ABOUT FEELING GOOD.

☐ Sickness is a *thief.* It steals time from those you love. It steals *money* that could be used to achieve your goals. It steals *energy* necessary to complete God's plan in your life.

☐ God wants you *well*. Get excited over it. The Great Physician is putting you back together.

☐ *Decide* to be healthy. *Decide* to feel good. *Decide* to be well.

WISDOM WORDS

"Surely He hath borne our griefs, and carried our sorrows: yet we did esteem Him stricken, smitten of God, and afflicted. But He was wounded for our transgressions, He was bruised for our iniquities: the chastisement of our peace was upon Him; and with His stripes we are healed."   Isaiah 53:4-5

VISUALIZE YOUR MIRACLE.

- ❑ *God begins every miracle with a mind-photograph.* This is normal. Every architect draws a picture before the building begins.

- ❑ Abraham visualized his generations of children every time he beheld the stars at night.

- ❑ Use your *memory. Replay* past victories. Use your *imagination* to *pre-play* in your mind those miracles that your heart has desired from the Lord. David did this and defeated the giant, Goliath. Champions.

WISDOM WORDS

"And He brought him forth abroad, and said, Look now toward heaven, and tell the stars, if thou be able to number them: and He said unto him, So shall thy seed be."   Genesis 15:5

NEVER QUIT REACHING.

❑ *Warfare will always surround the birth of your miracle.*

❑ Champions make the extra effort to *try one more time.*

❑ Miracles are not for the holy, they are for the *hungry.* The grapes of God's blessings are not placed within your mouth, but *within your reach. Don't quit until* you get what you want from God.

WISDOM WORDS

"The Lord is good unto them that wait for Him, to the soul that seeketh Him." Lamentations 3:25

TARGET YOUR SEED-FAITH.

❑ *Your tithes and offerings are Seeds that you sow.*
Seed-Faith is sowing what you have been *given* to
create something you have been *promised*.

❑ Elijah taught the Seed-Faith principle to the widow
of Zarephath. She believed it. She planted a portion
of what she had back into the work of God. She
expected her "Seed" to be multiplied back to her. It
happened.

❑ Plant a Seed today into the work of God. *Wrap your
faith around it* and remember that the Seed that
leaves your hand *really never leaves your life*. It goes
into your *future* where it *multiplies*.

WISDOM WORDS

"Bring ye all the tithes into the storehouse, that there
may be meat in Mine house, and prove Me now herewith,
saith the Lord of hosts, if I will not open you the windows
of heaven, and pour you out a blessing, that there shall
not be room enough to receive it."   Malachi 3:10

PRAY FOR SOMEONE ELSE.

❑ One of the Master Keys to personal miracles is to *get involved with the needs of others.*

❑ Joseph used his gift of interpreting dreams to calm a tormented Pharaoh. He was promoted from the prison to the palace. Job prayed for his friends during the worst crisis of his life. It released God to *reverse the curse.*

❑ God's contribution to you is always determined by what you have chosen to contribute to *others*. *What you make happen for others, God will make happen for you* (Eph. 6:8).

―― *WISDOM WORDS* ――

"And the Lord turned the captivity of Job, when he prayed for his friends: also the Lord gave Job twice as much as he had before."   Job 42:10

PROMOTE THE POWER OF JESUS.

❑ The first two letters of the word "gospel" spell…"GO."

❑ Christianity is a *network of activity*. Promote Jesus today. He is the Starting-Point of every miracle. Be the bridge that connects Him to somebody in trouble today.

❑ Be bold. *One miracle is worth a thousand sermons.*

WISDOM WORDS

"Go ye into all the world, and preach the gospel to every creature. And these signs shall follow them that believe; In My name shall they cast out devils; they shall speak with new tongues; They shall take up serpents; and if they drink any deadly thing, it shall not hurt them; they shall lay hands on the sick, and they shall recover."

Mark 16:15,17,18

BELIEVE THAT GOD WANTS YOU TO PROSPER.

❑ One of the many names of God is Jehovah-Jireh, "God will provide." Never doubt the giving nature of your Father.

❑ *You matter* to Him. Your *needs* matter to Him. Every *desire* of your heart is important to Him.

❑ Your total prosperity is on His mind all the time.

WISDOM WORDS

"Let them shout for joy, and be glad, that favour My righteous cause: yea, let them say continually, Let the Lord be magnified, which hath pleasure in the prosperity of His servant."   Psalm 35:27

EMBRACE TRUE PROSPERITY.

❑ Don't misunderstand "prosperity." Your *future* depends on it.

❑ Let's define it. Prosperity is simply *having enough of God's provisions to complete His instructions for your life.*

❑ Prosperity increases your ability to bless others.

WISDOM WORDS

"Beloved, I wish above all things that thou mayest prosper and be in health, even as thy soul prospereth."

3 John 1:2

WASH YOUR MIND WITH THE WORD.

❑ The Bible is God's Blueprint for mankind. It defines His purpose for creating, as well as His covenant to bless us.

❑ God promised that meditation on His words would produce the miracle of prosperity.

❑ *Nothing will ever dominate your life that doesn't happen daily.* (So, meditate on His Word, daily.)

❑ One of your great discoveries will be the Principle of Seed-Faith.

— *WISDOM WORDS* —

"That he might sanctify and cleanse it with the washing of water by the word," Ephesians 5:26

"Keep therefore the words of this covenant, and do them, that ye may prosper in all that ye do."
Deuteronomy 29:9

RESPECT THE LAW OF SOWING AND REAPING.

❑ When a farmer plants corn, he reaps corn. When he plants apple seeds, he produces more apples.

❑ When you sow love, you will reap love. If you sow hatred, you will reap the Harvest of hatred.

❑ This Scriptural Law of Sowing and Reaping is universal. Fools *deny* it. Rebels *defy* it. The wise *live by it.*

WISDOM WORDS

"Be not deceived; God is not mocked: for whatsoever a man soweth, that shall he also reap." Galatians 6:7

UNLOCK YOUR FUTURE.

❑ Seed-Faith is *exchanging* what you have been *given* for what God has *promised* you.

❑ Seed-Faith is sowing a Seed *in faith* for a specific Harvest.

❑ Seed-Faith *pulls the future toward you*.

WISDOM WORDS

"Give, and it shall be given unto you; good measure, pressed down, and shaken together, and running over, shall men give into your bosom. For with the same measure that ye mete withal it shall be measured to you again." Luke 6:38

NAME YOUR SEED.

❑ Inventory your *total* possessions.

❑ Everyone has *something* to give or sow.

❑ Your Seed is anything you have that will benefit another person, your *smile*...a *word* of encouragement...*time*...shared *information*... *money*.

WISDOM WORDS

"As every man hath received the gift, even so minister the same one to another, as good stewards of the manifold grace of God."   1 Peter 4:10

GET EXCITED ABOUT YOUR HUNDRED-FOLD RETURN.

❑ Jesus always promised a reward for any act of obedience.

❑ Start sowing your Seed with expectation of His blessing.

❑ Don't treat the promise of "hundred-fold" return lightly. It is your Father's opportunity to celebrate your faith.

WISDOM WORDS

"And Jesus answered and said, Verily I say unto you, There is no man that hath left house, or brethren, or sisters, or father, or mother, or wife, or children, or lands, for My sake, and the gospel's, But he shall receive an hundredfold now in this time, houses, and brethren, and sisters, and mothers, and children, and lands, with persecutions; and in the world to come eternal life."

Mark 10:29-30

ASK FOR A SPECIFIC HARVEST.

❑ Your Seed is whatever you give to God.

❑ Your Harvest is whatever God gives to you.

❑ Name the particular miracle you want from God.

WISDOM WORDS

"Be careful for nothing; but in every thing by prayer and supplication with thanksgiving let your requests be made known unto God."　　Philippians 4:6

RECOGNIZE YOUR HARVEST.

- ❑ Your Harvest is any *person* or *anything* that can bless or benefit you.

- ❑ It may be someone who can *contribute* something to you that you *need*...information...favor...finances... or it can be an explosive *idea*.

- ❑ Your Harvest *already* exists. It is walking around you! Just as your eyes had to be opened to recognize *Jesus,* your eyes must be opened to recognize your *Harvest*.

WISDOM WORDS

"He was in the world, and the world was made by Him, and the world knew Him not. He came unto His own, and His own received Him not."   John 1:10-11

RECOGNIZE YOUR SEED.

❑ Your Seed is any gift, skill or talent that God has provided for you, to sow into the lives of others.

❑ Don't hide it. *Use* it. Celebrate it. It carves the road to your future.

❑ Even Joseph wanted others to recognize his ability to interpret dreams.

— *WISDOM WORDS* —

"A man's gift maketh room for him, and bringeth him before great men."   Proverbs 18:16

START GIVING YOUR WAY OUT OF TROUBLE.

☐ Your Seed is always your *bridge* out of trouble.

☐ The widow of Zarephath used her Seed to create a Harvest in the midst of a famine. Joseph used his gift of interpreting dreams to catapult himself from the prison to the palace.

☐ *Whatever God has placed in your hand is always enough to get you out of trouble.*

WISDOM WORDS

"Neglect not the gift that is in thee, which was given thee by prophecy, with the laying on of the hands of the presbytery."   1 Timothy 4:14

HONOR THE TITHE.

- ❑ Tithing is the Biblical practice of *returning* ten percent of your income back to God after you have earned it.

- ❑ In the Old Testament, Abraham tithed. In the New Testament, even the Pharasees' tithing was noted by Jesus.

- ❑ Make God your financial partner. *Make every payday a Seed-Sowing Day.* Results are *guaranteed*.

— *WISDOM WORDS* —

"And all the tithe of the land, whether of the seed of the land, or of the fruit of the tree, is the Lord's: it is holy unto the Lord. And concerning the tithe of the herd, or of the flock, even of whatsoever passeth under the rod, the tenth shall be holy unto the Lord."

Leviticus 27:30,32

PAY YOUR VOWS.

❑ Always honor your promises to the Lord. It is also important that you honor your word to those in your family or business transactions.

❑ God is a Covenant-God. He seriously weighs every vow you have made before Him or man.

❑ Stop. Re-examine your past vows. Pay them. It positions you for *reward*.

WISDOM WORDS

"When thou vowest a vow unto God, defer not to pay it; for He hath no pleasure in fools: pay that which thou hast vowed. Better is it that thou shouldest not vow, than that thou shouldest vow and not pay."

Ecclesiastes 5:4,5

BREAK THE FINANCIAL CURSE.

- ❏ Those who rob God of the tithe and offerings that belong to Him live under a curse.

- ❏ *You can break "the Curse."* As you sow today, remember that your Seed is proof that you have conquered greed.

- ❏ God penalizes a thief, but always promotes and prospers the Seed-Sower.

WISDOM WORDS

"Will a man rob God? Yet ye have robbed Me. But ye say, Wherein have we robbed thee? In tithes and offerings. Ye are cursed with a curse: for ye have robbed Me, even this whole nation. Bring ye all the tithes into the storehouse, that there may be meat in Mine house, and prove Me now herewith, saith the Lord of hosts, if I will not open you the windows of heaven, and pour you out a blessing, that there shall not be room enough to receive it."   Malachi 3:8-10

OPEN YOUR HAND AND GOD WILL OPEN HIS HAND.

❑ Whatever you have in *your* hand is a Seed.

❑ Whatever God has in *His hand* is your Harvest.

❑ Nothing leaves Heaven until something leaves earth.

❑ Don't let fear and unbelief make you close your hands and hoard. Open your hands today, and God will pour out the greatest blessings you have ever experienced.

— *WISDOM WORDS* —

"Bring ye all the tithes into the storehouse, that there may be meat in Mine house, and prove Me now herewith, saith the Lord of hosts, if I will not open you the windows of heaven, and pour you out a blessing, that there shall not be room enough to receive it. And I will rebuke the devourer for your sakes, and he shall not destroy the fruits of your ground; neither shall your vine cast her fruit before the time in the field, saith the Lord of hosts."
Malachi 3:10-11

RELEASE THE HOLY SPIRIT TO BRING YOUR HARVEST.

❑ The Holy Spirit can *go* where you cannot go. The Holy Spirit can *say* what you cannot say. The Holy Spirit can *do* what you cannot do.

❑ You can pray in your city…the Holy Spirit will talk to someone 2,000 miles away.

❑ *Honor the Holy Spirit.* Permit Him to *move.* Don't quench Him. He is the *movement* of the Seed-faith principle.

WISDOM WORDS

"That they should seek the Lord, if haply they might feel after Him, and find Him, though He be not far from every one of us: For in Him we live, and move, and have our being; as certain also of your own poets have said, For we are also His offspring." Acts 17:27,28

TAKE THE LIMITS OFF OF GOD.

❑ *Anytime you attempt to do the impossible, you will create a crisis.* These are the seasons that pleasure God…for this allows Him to *reveal* Himself…His power…and His love.

❑ You serve a *big* God…so, make *BIG* plans. He delights in *proving* His power to you.

❑ This is the secret of Seed-faith: Whatever you have in your hand is what God will use to create your future. *Don't limit God. Anything is possible.*

WISDOM WORDS

"…But the people that do know their God shall be strong, and do exploits."   Daniel 11:32

DON'T TOLERATE LACK.

❑ Poverty is *wrenching*...tortuous...tormenting. It strips a person of the ability to give...to bless...to make a contribution to others. *Don't tolerate it.*

❑ Learn to despise lack. *You will never conquer what you cannot hate.*

❑ Your Seed is the *Enemy of Lack.* It is the only proof that you truly desire a Harvest.

WISDOM WORDS

"And God is able to make all grace abound toward you; that ye, always having all sufficiency in all things, may abound to every good work:" 2 Corinthians 9:8

EXPLORE NEW INCOME POSSIBILITIES.

❑ You are *not* locked into your present job. You have *chosen* to be where you are. You can *choose* to be somewhere else.

❑ *Seasons* change. *Companies* change. *You* change. *Accept it.* Enjoy your God-given right to creatively pursue and explore other job opportunities.

❑ Most Assignments are *seasonal.* Permit God to walk you into the *next* chapter of success in your life.

WISDOM WORDS

"Behold, I will do a new thing; now it shall spring forth; shall ye not know it? I will even make a way in the wilderness, and rivers in the desert." Isaiah 43:19

BUILD YOUR BUDGET WITH FAITH.

- ❑ Your budget is simply a *written* Plan for Spending. It is the secret of every Financial Champion.

- ❑ Your Financial World is decided by three factors: (1) what you *spend*, (2) what you *save*, and (3) what you *sow*.

- ❑ When you put God *first* in tithes and offerings, you are building your budget on Foundation of *Faith*...for the *Rest* of your needs to be met.

WISDOM WORDS

"But seek ye first the kingdom of God, and His righteousness; and all these things shall be added unto you."   Matthew 6:33

ACCEPT THE SEED THAT GOD SOWED.

- ❑ God had a Son. He wanted a *family*. Like a Seed, He planted His Son. The place was called *Calvary*.

- ❑ God lost what He loved...*for a Season*, to produce *more* of what He loved...you and me.

- ❑ Jesus is the Seed within you that reproduces the nature of God. Accept Him now as Savior... Lord...King of your life.

WISDOM WORDS

"For ye know the grace of our Lord Jesus Christ, that, though He was rich, yet for your sakes He became poor, that ye through His poverty might be rich."

2 Corinthians 8:9

BECOME SOMEONE'S HARVEST.

❑ *What you are, you will reproduce around you.* The Irishman produces Irishmen. The apple produces more apples. The giver creates givers...who want to contribute into his life.

❑ What appears to be a *loss* today will prove to be a *gain* tomorrow.

❑ *You are a Seed.* Sow yourself into the future. Sow yourself into someone else. You are somebody's Harvest today. Find them.

WISDOM WORDS

"Give, and it shall be given unto you; good measure, pressed down, and shaken together, and running over, shall men give into your bosom. For with the same measure that ye mete withal it shall be measured to you again." Luke 6:38

GIVE YOURSELF AWAY.

❑ You are a collection of *parts.* When you sow a *part* of yourself back in God's world, you activate the *Law of Increase.*

❑ Sow extra *time* into your family and you will see an *increase* of love and affection. Sow the Seed of *diligence* into your job and you will be *promoted.*

❑ Start giving yourself away. After all, *everything you have was given to you.*

WISDOM WORDS

"Heal the sick, cleanse the lepers, raise the dead, cast out devils: freely ye have received, freely give."

Matthew 10:8

FIND SOMEBODY IN TROUBLE.

❑ *Everyone hurts somewhere.*

❑ You are oil for someone's wounds. You are the map for someone who is lost. *Find them. God is always willing to become to you, whatever you are willing to become to another.*

❑ Remember you are a Seed. Sow yourself. Never forget: *What you make happen for others, God will make happen for you.*

WISDOM WORDS

"And if thou draw out thy soul to the hungry, and satisfy the afflicted soul; then shall thy light rise in obscurity, and thy darkness be as the noon day: And the Lord shall guide thee continually, and satisfy thy soul in drought, and make fat thy bones: and thou shalt be like a watered garden, and like a spring of water, whose waters fail not."   Isaiah 58:10-11

SOW MERCY; EXPECT MERCY.

❑ *Forgiveness is a Seed.* Sow it generously, and you will reap it generously.

❑ Each offense from others is actually an *opportunity*. It is your chance to create *favor* with man…and God.

❑ *Your Heavenly Father will never give to you what you refuse to give to others.* Mercy-People *attract* mercy into their lives.

WISDOM WORDS

"For if ye forgive men their trespasses, your heavenly Father will also forgive you: But if ye forgive not men their trespasses, neither will your Father forgive your trespasses."   Matthew 6:14-15

FIGHT FOR YOUR HARVEST.

- ❏ You have an Enemy. An Adversary. A Thief. Satan wants to steal everything God has for you. Don't let him!

- ❏ Use your weapons to go after the Harvest when it has been delayed. Your *weapons* are the *Word of God,* your *words* and your *faith*.

- ❏ God *responds* to a fighter. Satan *fears* a fighter. *Every Harvest in your life will require a battle.*

WISDOM WORDS

"Blessed be the Lord my strength, which teacheth my hands to war, and my fingers to fight:"   Psalm 144:1

START CREATING TOMORROW...TODAY.

❑ A farmer begins sowing his seeds months *before* he needs the harvest. There is a *time* for *sowing*...a *time* for *reaping*.

❑ Tomorrow is being decided right now. Your Seeds of love...mercy...money...are *moving into your future*.

❑ *The Seed that leaves your hand will never leave your life*. It merely leaves your *present* season, and *enters your future* where it multiplies.

WISDOM WORDS

"To every thing there is a season, and a time to every purpose under the heaven: A time to be born, and a time to die; a time to plant, and a time to pluck up that which is planted;"   Ecclesiastes 3:1,2

DON'T FORGET YOUR SOURCE.

- ❑ Everything you need comes *from* God...*through* people. He is your Source. Men are His *channels*.

- ❑ God may use various people to benefit you. But, never forget to be thankful and grateful to the True Source—your Heavenly Father.

- ❑ *Read* the word of God aloud. *Speak* it aloud. It builds your confidence and faith in God.

WISDOM WORDS

"But without faith it is impossible to please Him; for he that cometh to God must believe that He is, and that He is a rewarder of them that diligently seek Him."

Hebrews 11:6

ESTABLISH A RHYTHM IN YOUR SOWING AND REAPING.

❑ Acknowledge the fact of the Seasons…Winter, Spring, Summer, Fall. Regularity and routine are very important forces in your life…especially, in a Seed-faith lifestyle.

❑ Your life is an endless cycle of sowing and reaping; giving and receiving. *Work with it*. Don't be erratic and unpredictable. Nature itself has a rhythm…a pattern. Honor it.

❑ Create a personal schedule for sowing your finances into God's work. This will create a *rhythm* and *consistency* in the Harvests you receive from God.

— *WISDOM WORDS* —

"While the earth remaineth, seedtime and harvest, and cold and heat, and summer and winter, and day and night shall not cease."   Genesis 8:22

CONQUER GREED.

- ❑ Satan *steals.* Man *hoards.* God *gives.* Your giving is the only proof that God lives within you. Whether it is money, mercy or love. *Giving is the only real evidence of love.*

- ❑ Your Seed is the only proof that you have conquered greed. It will be God's biggest memory for you today.

- ❑ Receiving establishes your limits. *Sowing takes the limits off.* That's why Jesus said that it is more *advantageous* and *productive* to *give*…than to receive. When you unleash your Seed…you unleash the potential of your *future.*

WISDOM WORDS

"…It is more blessed to give than to receive."

Acts 20:35

MAKE UP YOUR MIND TO OVERCOME.

❑ Job is a great example of persistence in the midst of human suffering. He was stripped financially. His children were killed. His closest friends judged him guilty of some hidden sin. But, he *determined to overcome*.

❑ The *opinions of others will never change your character*. Ultimately and inevitably, integrity wins. *Always*.

❑ Whatever the price, overcoming is worth it.

WISDOM WORDS

"Though He slay me, yet will I trust in Him: but I will maintain mine own ways before Him."   Job 13:15

CHOOSE TO CONQUER.

❑ Many have faced adversity greater than your own. *Yet, they overcame.* Their secret was that they *chose* to conquer.

❑ *Stop looking for excuses to fail.* Start looking for reasons to *succeed. Overcoming is a choice.*

❑ The Apostle Paul received 195 lashes with a whip... beaten 3 times with rods...stoned and left for dead... shipwrecked 3 times...yet the world has never forgotten him. *He chose to conquer.*

WISDOM WORDS

"Who shall separate us from the love of Christ? shall tribulation, or distress, or persecution, or famine, or nakedness, or peril, or sword? Nay, in all these things we are more than conquerors through Him that loved us."   Romans 8:35,37

CULTIVATE THE MENTALITY OF AN OVERCOMER.

❑ Champions *think* differently. They refuse to waste their energy and thoughts on their obstacles. Instead, they concentrate on their *goals*.

❑ You, too, can change your thought-life. It may take a little time, but it is well worth it.

❑ Fix your mind on Portraits of Victories you will experience. Now...*Move Toward Them.*

WISDOM WORDS

"Finally, brethren, whatsoever things are true, whatsoever things are honest, whatsoever things are just, whatsoever things are pure, whatsoever things are lovely, whatsoever things are of good report; if there be any virtue, and if there be any praise, think on these things." Philippians 4:8

FACE YOUR PROBLEMS HONESTLY.

❏ Don't blame others for what *you* have chosen to do. Don't blame others for the *consequences* of your choices. *Never complain about what you permit.*

❏ Your life is the *result of your choices.*

❏ *Name your weaknesses.* Nobody else can do it. Nobody else *will* do it. Nobody else *should have* to do it. Your honesty will determine your victories.

WISDOM WORDS

"If we say that we have no sin, we deceive ourselves, and the truth is not in us. If we confess our sins, He is faithful and just to forgive us our sins, and to cleanse us from all unrighteousness."   1 John 1:8-9

STORE UP POWER.

❑ The Word of God has *power*. When Jesus faced the tempter (Matthew 4), He quoted the Scriptures to *thwart* satan. *It worked*. Jesus won.

❑ Discipline yourself for the next 30 days to read one chapter a day. Begin with the book of Acts.

❑ It is the Power-Book of the Bible. *Store it up* within you. Prayer produces *joy*. The Word produces *power*. Do both *daily. Nothing will ever dominate your life unless it happens daily.*

WISDOM WORDS

"For the word of God is quick, and powerful, and sharper than any twoedged sword, piercing even to the dividing asunder of soul and spirit, and of the joints and marrow, and is a discerner of the thoughts and intents of the heart."   Hebrews 4:12

LEARN THE ART OF ATTACK.

❑ Overcomers are *not* passive. They *pursue*. They cannot tolerate enslavement.

❑ *What you fail to master will eventually master you.* It may be anger, an addiction or an attitude.

❑ *Target* your enemy. *God loves a fighter.* Paul attacked tradition. Jesus attacked sickness and disease. Go ahead...learn the joy of attack.

WISDOM WORDS

"Blessed be the Lord my strength, which teacheth my hands to war, and my fingers to fight:"   Psalm 144:1

KNOW YOUR OPPONENT.

❑ Satan is your *real* adversary. He is a *fallen* angel, dispelled from Heaven by a righteous God.

❑ Satan's methods are predictable. He *incites* the violent nature of men against you. He *inflames* the normal passions of man into perversion. He *introduces* thoughts that could ultimately destroy you.

❑ Satan reacts to the *spoken* Word of God. He is easily demoralized with the *Weapon of Praise.* He flees when you *resist* him.

— *WISDOM WORDS* —

"For we wrestle not against flesh and blood, but against principalities, against powers, against the rulers of the darkness of this world, against spiritual wickedness in high places."　　　　　　　　　　　Ephesians 6:12

UNLEASH THE HOLY SPIRIT WITHIN YOU.

❑ The Holy Spirit is a *Person*. A *Teacher*. A *Companion*. He is the *Presence* and the *Power* of God.

❑ Before The Experience, Peter was cowardly, denying Jesus Christ. *After* The Experience, he won thousands to Christ instead.

❑ *Obey* the voice of the Holy Spirit within you...*hourly*. Don't take His instructions lightly. *Each instruction is linked to an event in your future.*

WISDOM WORDS

"But ye shall receive power, after that the Holy Ghost is come upon you: and ye shall be witnesses unto Me both in Jerusalem, and in all Judaea, and in Samaria, and unto the uttermost part of the earth."   Acts 1:8

LISTEN TO PAIN.

❑ Pain is *discomfort created by disorder.* It is *not* really an enemy. It is a *signal,* a *memo,* a *messenger* telling you an enemy exists.

❑ When you were a child, you may have touched a hot iron. It hurt! Pain made you jerk your hand away… *make changes*…to *protect* yourself from injury.

❑ If things are going wrong in your life, take it seriously. *Pain talks.* Initiate any *change* that may be necessary.

WISDOM WORDS

"…weeping may endure for a night, but joy cometh in the morning."   Psalm 30:5

USE THE WEAPON OF PRAISE.

❑ King Saul was often tormented by evil spirits. When this happened, he called for David, the Psalmist and shepherd boy, to play the harp. The evil spirits always departed.

❑ *Praise and worship are dreaded weapons in hell.* Demon powers are demoralized by it.

❑ *Don't neglect this weapon.* It is too powerful to ignore. As you lift your hands in worship and praise, you will literally *purge the atmosphere* of demonic activity.

WISDOM WORDS

"And it came to pass, when the evil spirit from God was upon Saul, that David took an harp, and played with his hand: so Saul was refreshed, and was well, and the evil spirit departed from him." 1 Samuel 16:23

RECOGNIZE YOUR DELIVERER.

❑ God *assigns* Deliverers. Moses was *assigned* to lead the Israelites out of Egypt. Elijah was *sent* to the widow of Zarephath to help her use her faith for provision.

❑ If you are sick, *look* for the man of God who believes in *healing*. If you are having financial problems, *look* for the man of God who *believes in prosperity*.

❑ *No one fails alone.* If you fail, it will be because you *chose to ignore those God assigned to help you*.

WISDOM WORDS

"O Jerusalem, Jerusalem, thou that killest the prophets, and stonest them which are sent unto thee, how often would I have gathered thy children together, even as a hen gathereth her chickens under her wings, and ye would not! Behold, your house is left unto you desolate."
Matthew 23:37-38

REACH FOR HELP.

❑ *Reaching out for help is not a sign of weakness.* So, do it. Only a fool ignores a life-jacket when he is drowning.

❑ *Overcomers don't do it alone.* They conquer their pride. They reject the *trap of isolation.* They *reach.* They *know* the inevitable reward of reaching.

❑ *Turn to God.* Honor those who are qualified to help you. *Your future depends on it.*

WISDOM WORDS

"When thou art in tribulation, and all these things are come upon thee, even in the latter days, if thou turn to the Lord thy God, and shalt be obedient unto His voice; For the Lord thy God is a merciful God; He will not forsake thee, neither destroy thee, nor forget the covenant of thy fathers which He sware unto them."

Deuteronomy 4:30-31

TALK LIKE A VICTOR, NOT A VICTIM.

❑ Your words are *signals...scents.* They can be like the fragrance of a rose or the odor of a skunk. They can *attract or repel.*

❑ *Don't talk like a "victim."* It invites pity, but not partnership. Even in the animal kingdom the wounded are attacked, not assisted.

❑ Your words are continually *educating* others around you. Let them create a portrait of enthusiasm and faith.

WISDOM WORDS

"Death and life are in the power of the tongue: and they that love it shall eat the fruit thereof."

Proverbs 18:21

ENDURE. ENDURE. ENDURE.

❑ *Overcoming involves more than one battle.* The man who *refuses* to quit…always wins. *Always.*

❑ The mysterious, invisible quality of a Champion is *endurance*. They refuse to run from a fight. They *insist* on one more round.

❑ *Don't ever consider quitting.* Get up and try again. And, again. And, *again*. Hell fears a fighter.

WISDOM WORDS

"Blessed is the man that endureth temptation: for when he is tried, he shall receive the crown of life, which the Lord hath promised to them that love Him."

James 1:12

DON'T NEGLECT YOUR SPIRITUAL ARMOR.

- ❑ It is *invisible*. It is *overlooked*. Yet, like air, it still exists. As a soldier in the army of God, *you must put on your spiritual armor* during your morning prayer time.

- ❑ Pray this prayer: "Father, I wrap Your *Truth* around my lions. I wear the breastplate of Your *Righteousness*. My feet walk in Your *Peace*. I take the *Shield of Faith*. I wear the helmet of *Salvation*. Your *Word* will be the weapon in my mouth today, the *Sword of the Spirit*. I wear the protection of Your armor and nothing shall harm me in any way today."

- ❑ Believe me, this armor, though invisible to *you*, is highly apparent to satan, your enemy. *Put it on*.

WISDOM WORDS

"Put on the whole armour of God, that ye may be able to stand against the wiles of the devil."   Ephesians 6:11

USE YOUR PRAYER LANGUAGE.

❑ Millions are discovering the remarkable secret of praying in the Spirit...*praying in an unknown language.* The Apostle Paul did it. You can, too.

❑ *Become uninhibited* in your prayer life. Permit the Heavenly language to flow out of you toward the Father.

❑ Talk to God about this supernatural experience. It is one of the most effective tools in the life of an Overcomer. *Use it.*

— *WISDOM WORDS* —

"Likewise the Spirit also helpeth our infirmities: for we know not what we should pray for as we ought: but the Spirit itself maketh intercession for us with groanings which cannot be uttered. And He that searcheth the hearts knoweth what is the mind of the Spirit, because He maketh intercession for the saints according to the will of God."   Romans 8:26-27

"But ye, beloved, building up yourselves on your most holy faith, praying in the Holy Ghost,"   Jude 1:20

EXPECT SUPERNATURAL INTERVENTION.

❑ Elisha and his servant were surrounded by Syrian soldiers. The servant, trembling with fear, cried, "Alas, my master! How shall we do?"

❑ Elisha answered, "Fear not: for they that be with us are more than they that be with them." The servant's eyes were opened and he saw the invisible army of angels *supernaturally assigned* to protect them.

❑ *Expect the Supernatural.* Angels are assigned to you. Never underestimate the attentiveness of your Father. *Nothing is ever as bad as it first appears.*

— WISDOM WORDS —

"He giveth power to the faint; and to them that have no might He increaseth strength." Isaiah 40:29

"And Elisha prayed, and said, Lord, I pray thee, open his eyes, that he may see. And the Lord opened the eyes of the young man; and he saw: and, behold, the mountain was full of horses and chariots of fire round about Elisha." 2 Kings 6:17

REFUSE TO FEAR.

- ❏ *Fear attracts attack.* Even animals have been known to attack humans when they have sensed fear.

- ❏ Fear is the *feeling of anticipated loss.* It may be loss of reputation, property, love, health or life.

- ❏ *Loss is not fatal.* First, everything you presently possess was given to you by God. Second, whatever you have given back to God cannot be stolen by man. Third, anything man has ever taken from you, God has promised to restore.

WISDOM WORDS

"And I will restore to you the years that the locust hath eaten, the cankerworm, and the caterpiller, and the palmerworm, My great army which I sent among you."
Joel 2:25

"For God hath not given us the spirit of fear; but of power, and of love, and of a sound mind."

2 Timothy 1:7

RISK EVERYTHING TO BE AN OVERCOMER.

❑ *Overcomers are the Rewarded.* In fact, they are the *only* ones who are rewarded through eternity.

❑ Even the Apostle Paul counted everything as loss *except* his position with Christ. *Each victory authorizes God to promote you.*

❑ In the World System, *birth* may decide rank. In the Kingdom System, *battle* decides rank. *Every satanic attack upon you is simply another opportunity for promotion.*

WISDOM WORDS

"I have fought a good fight, I have finished my course, I have kept the faith: Henceforth there is laid up for me a crown of righteousness, which the Lord, the righteous judge, shall give me at that day: and not to me only, but unto all them also that love His appearing."

2 Timothy 4:7-8

GROW YOUR FAITH.

☐ *Everything begins small.* The oak tree began with an acorn. The skyscraper began with a brick.

☐ Even weightlifters started their careers with just a few pounds. Little by little, they birthed new levels of strength and power.

☐ *Water the Seeds of Faith* in your heart. Give them a chance to grow. *You are just a portion of what you will be tomorrow.*

WISDOM WORDS

"For who hath despised the day of small things"
Zechariah 4:10

"Though thy beginning was small, yet thy latter end should greatly increase." Job 8:7

WAKE UP THE SEED OF GOD WITHIN YOU.

❑ *You are the offspring of a perfect God.* This explains your appetite for order, excellence and perfection.

❑ *You are the offspring of a warring God.* This explains your warfare with satan and evil.

❑ *You are the offspring of an overcoming God.* So, wake up the dormant Seed within you. Release His Holy Spirit to work through you today.

WISDOM WORDS

"Ye are of God, little children, and have overcome them: because greater is He that is in you, than he that is in the world." 1 John 4:4

RUN TO THE REFUGE.

❑ Cities of refuge existed in Old Testament times. If a man was accused of a crime, he could run into a city of refuge and was guaranteed protection by law.

❑ You, too, have a Place of Refuge. When satan the accuser, brings accusations against your life, *run to God*.

❑ God responds to *reachers. Stop looking at where you have been, and start looking at where you can be.* Run to the Refuge. Do it today.

WISDOM WORDS

"For Thou hast been a strength to the poor, a strength to the needy in his distress, a refuge from the storm, a shadow from the heat, when the blast of the terrible ones is as a storm against the wall."   Isaiah 25:4

SOW A BATTLE-SEED.

❑ Your Seed is anything you do that helps another. It may be information, encouragement, or even finances. Whatever it is, *Your Seed Is Always Your Door Out Of Trouble.*

❑ Job sowed a prayer of deliverance for his three friends. *Then*, God turned Job's captivity around. David stopped a tragedy by offering a special offering to the Lord.

❑ *Your contribution to someone in trouble always unlocks God's contribution back into your life.*

WISDOM WORDS

"And David built there an altar unto the Lord, and offered burnt offerings and peace offerings. So the Lord was entreated for the land, and the plague was stayed from Israel."   2 Samuel 24:25

"Give, and it shall be given unto you; good measure, pressed down, and shaken together, and running over, shall men give into your bosom. For with the same measure that ye mete withal it shall be measured to you again."   Luke 6:38

KEEP YOUR FOCUS.

❏ The Secret of Success is *concentration.* The Secret of Failure is *broken focus.*

❏ The forbidden fruit *distracted* Adam and Eve. Delilah *distracted* Samson. *Whatever takes your mind away from God's Assignment is an instrument of Hell.*

❏ Examine your life. Honestly. Disconnect from every distraction. *Fix your focus.* Don't let satan ever get a foot inside your door. *You are too close to Victory to lose out now.*

WISDOM WORDS

"Only be thou strong and very courageous, that thou mayest observe to do according to all the law, which Moses My servant commanded thee: turn not from it to the right hand or to the left, that thou mayest prosper whithersoever thou goest."   Joshua 1:7

REMEMBER THE TREE OF LIFE.

❑ *Overcomers are ultimately rewarded.* Even the Apostle Paul anticipated a crown of righteousness.

❑ Don't forfeit Heaven for one weak moment. Too much is at stake.

❑ *Heaven is waiting.* A parade of celebration is about to begin. *Keep your eyes on paradise.* The grandstands of Heaven are full of champions who have gone on before you. *Remember.*

WISDOM WORDS

"He that hath an ear, let him hear what the Spirit saith unto the churches; To him that overcometh will I give to eat of the tree of life, which is in the midst of the paradise of God."   Revelation 2:7

REMEMBER THE CROWN OF LIFE.

- ❑ *Overcoming is not a small thing to God*. He celebrates faithfulness. Forever.

- ❑ Don't give in to satan today. *In anything.* You are too close to your Rewards.

- ❑ A moment of pain is worth an eternity of gain. *Go for the Crown!*

WISDOM WORDS

"...be thou faithful unto death, and I will give thee a crown of life...He that overcometh shall not be hurt of the second death."   Revelation 2:10-11

REMEMBER THE WHITE STONE.

❑ You may be sorely tempted today. Satan may influence every appetite of your flesh. *Stay strong.*

❑ You are a Trophy of the grace of God. Hell is incensed over your loyalty to God.

❑ *Your Reward Ceremony is closer than you realize.* Hidden manna...a white stone...and your new name. Your happiness has just begun. *You are too close to Home to turn back now.*

WISDOM WORDS

"He that hath an ear, let him hear what the Spirit saith unto the churches; To him that overcometh will I give to eat of the hidden manna, and will give him a white stone, and in the stone a new name written, which no man knoweth saving he that receiveth it."

Revelation 2:17

REMEMBER YOUR RULERSHIP.

- ❑ *Overcomers are always on God's mind.* He has declared that He will turn the nations of the earth over to Overcomers.

- ❑ Don't weaken in The Battle Of Life today. *You are too close to promotion.* Every general knows that rulership is worth the price of discipline. Short-term pain for long-term gain.

- ❑ Each victory is a step toward the throne. A giant step. *You are closer than you have ever been to the Palace. Start acting like royalty.*

WISDOM WORDS

"And he that overcometh, and keepeth My works unto the end, to him will I give power over the nations: And he shall rule them with a rod of iron; as the vessels of a potter shall they be broken to shivers: even as I received of My Father. And I will give him the morning star."

Revelation 2:26-28

REMEMBER YOUR NAME IN THE BOOK OF LIFE.

❑ *God keeps a daily journal.* He records the names and victories of every one of His children.

❑ *Overcomers will never be blotted out of His Book.* The names of every overcomer will echo through the Chambers of Heaven. Angels will hear it.

❑ Get excited today about overcoming. You are stepping into the Arena of Champions. *Your name is becoming familiar in Heaven these days.*

WISDOM WORDS

"He that overcometh, the same shall be clothed in white raiment; and I will not blot out his name out of the book of life, but I will confess his name before My Father, and before His angels." Revelation 3:5

REMEMBER YOUR CITIZENSHIP.

❑ Earth is *temporary*. Eternity is *permanent*. You are a pilgrim here. This is a journey, a passage, a season. *The future is far more suited to you.*

❑ *You are a Citizen of the New Jerusalem.* You are an ambassador, a representative on earth of your Heavenly Father. *Don't ever forget it.*

❑ Overcomers are guaranteed a permanent place in the Temple of God. His Name is engraved upon You. You are His property and a perpetuation of His kingdom. *Act like the Royalty you are.*

WISDOM WORDS

"Him that overcometh will I make a pillar in the Temple of my God, and he shall go no more out: and I will write upon him the name of My God, and the name of the city of My God, which is new Jerusalem, which cometh down out of heaven from My God: and I will write upon him My new name." Revelation 3:12

REMEMBER YOU ARE ROYALTY.

❑ Overcomers are uncommon. Extraordinary. *Unforgettable.* They *think* differently. They act differently. They *talk* differently.

❑ Jesus was an Overcomer. And He promised to *elevate* every overcomer with *Himself!*

❑ *You Have Never Been Where You Are Going.* You have never known the honor you are going to experience. *Overcomers are royalty. An eternal banquet is being prepared for you even now.*

WISDOM WORDS

"To him that overcometh will I grant to sit with Me in My throne, even as I also overcame, and am set down with My Father in His throne."   Revelation 3:21

SEE HABIT AS A GIFT FROM GOD.

❑ A *habit* is any action, conduct or behavior that you do over and over again. It may be a *bad* habit like smoking, or a *good* habit like brushing your teeth.

❑ This means *anything you do twice becomes easier.* It is God's way of helping you succeed.

❑ Some experts believe that when you do a specific thing repeatedly 21 consecutive days, it will become a lifetime habit for you.

WISDOM WORDS

"Every good gift and every perfect gift is from above, and cometh down from the Father of lights, with Whom is no variableness, neither shadow of turning."

James 1:17

MAKE A LIST OF NEW HABITS.

❑ Brainstorm for *new* habits. Make up your bed *immediately* upon rising. Use a highlighter pen to mark your Bible each day.

❑ Hang up your clothes. Make a daily to-do list each morning. Limit each phone call to five minutes.

❑ Rise the *same time* every morning. Keep an idea notebook with you *at all times*. Write at least one sentence in your daily diary or journal.

WISDOM WORDS

"Write the vision, and make it plain upon tables, that he may run that readeth it." Habakkuk 2:2

EXAMINE SUCCESS HABITS OF CHAMPIONS.

❑ *Great men have great habits. Daily* habits. That is what separates them from the masses.

❑ Men do not really decide their future. They merely decided their habits. Then...their *habits* decide their future.

❑ Read biographies of champions. *The secret of their success is always hidden in something they do DAILY.*

WISDOM WORDS

"Now when Daniel knew that the writing was signed, he went into his house; and his windows being open in his chamber toward Jerusalem, he kneeled upon his knees three times a day, and prayed, and gave thanks before his God, as he did aforetime."   Daniel 6:10

NAME THE HABITS YOU MOST DESIRE.

- ❑ Take a sheet of paper. *List* those habits that make men unusually successful. Be honest.

- ❑ Specify those habits that could apply to *your* life and help you achieve your goals.

- ❑ Target *one* new habit this week. Now, believe that God will help you achieve it.

WISDOM WORDS

"And in that day ye shall ask Me nothing. Verily, verily, I say unto you, Whatsoever ye shall ask the Father in My name, He will give it you. Hitherto have ye asked nothing in My name: ask, and ye shall receive, that your joy may be full."   John 16:23-24

BEGIN A GOOD HABIT TODAY.

❑ *Decide to change.* Do it now.

❑ Make a change in something you do every day. *You will never really change your life until you change something you do daily.*

❑ *Choose* to develop the habits of champions. *Start a new one today.*

WISDOM WORDS

"Therefore if any man be in Christ, he is a new creature: old things are passed away; behold, all things are become new." 2 Corinthians 5:17

ALLOW YOURSELF TIME TO CHANGE.

❑ Don't be too hard on yourself. Little-by-little and day-by-day, you will start tasting the rewards of change.

❑ Look at the patience of God with Israel. He "knew they were but flesh." He took many years to even train their leader, Moses. You are not an exception.

❑ Every man fails. Champions simply get back up... and *begin again*.

WISDOM WORDS

"The Lord upholdeth all that fall, and raiseth up all those that be bowed down." Psalm 145:14

CONFRONT DESTRUCTIVE HABITS.

❑ Don't waste your life. It is too short, valuable and irreplaceable.

❑ Confront problems. *What you refuse to master today, will master you tomorrow.*

❑ Remember: *what you do habitually determines what you become permanently.* Get up. Fight back. You can *win.*

WISDOM WORDS

"Submit yourselves therefore to God. Resist the devil, and he will flee from you." James 4:7

DON'T DECEIVE YOURSELF.

❑ You already know the bad habits in your life. Face them. *You will never correct what you are unwilling to confront.*

❑ Resist the urge to justify yourself. *Truth is temporarily painful, but permanently liberating.*

❑ Change *is* possible. Step-by-step and day-by-day, start moving towards the dreams and goals of your life.

WISDOM WORDS

"Search me, O God, and know my heart: try me, and know my thoughts: And see if there be any wicked way in me, and lead me in the way everlasting."

Psalm 139:23-24

DESPISE YOUR CHAINS.

- ❑ You are a child of the Most High God. Captivity is *unnatural* for you. Learn to hate the chains of any habit that enslaves you.

- ❑ While drug addicts and alcoholics may want the *taste* of sin, they certainly do not want the *torment*. But they will never be free until they learn to *despise* those chains.

- ❑ Habit is hell's greatest weapon in destroying your life. *Let God break your chains.*

WISDOM WORDS

"The Spirit of the Lord God is upon me; because the Lord hath anointed me to preach good tidings unto the meek; He hath sent me to bind up the brokenhearted, to proclaim liberty to the captives, and the opening of the prison to them that are bound;"   Isaiah 61:1

"If the Son therefore shall make you free, ye shall be free indeed."   John 8:36

DIFFERENTIATE BETWEEN DISCIPLINE AND HABIT.

❑ Many people do not know the difference between *discipline* and *habit*.

❑ Discipline is forcing yourself to do something. It may be uncomfortable, unpleasant, even miserable in the beginning. *It is simply doing something you hate, to create something you love.*

❑ Habit is the child of discipline. It is something you do *naturally*, easily and without conscious effort. Champions become champions by *maintaining a discipline until it becomes a habit,* a daily routine in their lives.

WISDOM WORDS

"Evening, and morning, and at noon, will I pray, and cry aloud: and He shall hear my voice."   Psalm 55:17

PINPOINT YOUR LIFE-PURPOSE.

❑ Great habits are the results of great *purpose*.

❑ Let me explain. Mohammad Ali, the famous boxer, felt he was divinely appointed to become the heavyweight champion of the world. He felt he was born for *such a purpose*. This sense of purpose was his motivation to develop the daily workout *habits* that made him great.

❑ Always remember the powerful importance of *linking your habits to your life purpose.*

WISDOM WORDS

"But ye are a chosen generation, a royal priesthood, an holy nation, a peculiar people; that ye should shew forth the praises of Him Who hath called you out of darkness into His marvellous light:"   1 Peter 2:9

PERFECT YOUR DAILY SUCCESS ROUTINE.

❑ *The Secret Of Your Future Is Hidden In Your Daily Routine.*

❑ Daily tasks should be performed at the *same time* each day. Weekly tasks should be performed on the *same day* each week. Develop a *rhythm* to your life.

❑ Sit down now. Make your personal list of daily activities. Link each task to a specific time or day to be performed.

WISDOM WORDS

"And He came to Nazareth, where He had been brought up: and, *as His custom was,* He went into the synagogue on the sabbath day, and stood up for to read."

Luke 4:16

EXERCISE EVERY DAY.

❑ Health is life's First Prize. *Good health* is a product of good habits.

❑ *Make the effort.* Schedule 30 minutes each day for exercise. Take care of your body, and it will take care of you.

❑ Ask your close friends to help motivate you. Set achievable goals. *Just do it. TODAY.*

— *WISDOM WORDS* —

"What? know ye not that your body is the temple of the Holy Ghost which is in you, which ye have of God, and ye are not your own? For ye are bought with a price: therefore glorify God in your body, and in your spirit, which are God's."   1 Corinthians 6:19-20

ATTEND CHURCH FAITHFULLY.

❑ Get into the Presence of God. *Regularly.* Your best will come out of you in His Presence.

❑ Sit under the teaching of a man of God you respect. Put your time, influence and finances there. *Faithfully.*

❑ Even Jesus attended church regularly. There is no substitute for the Golden Link of Godly relationships.

— *WISDOM WORDS* —

"Not forsaking the assembling of ourselves together, as the manner of some is; but exhorting one another: and so much the more, as ye see the day approaching."
Hebrews 10:25

"...As His custom was, He went into the synagogue on the sabbath day..."
Luke 4:16

BEGIN THE BIBLE HABIT.

❑ Pick a time...preferably, the *morning*. Call it your "Wisdom-Hour." *Read the Bible aloud.*

❑ Don't get bogged down in theology, or the Greek and Hebrew translations. Just *meditate* on His Word.

❑ His Words is *life*. His Word creates *faith*. His Word will *change the course of your life.*

WISDOM WORDS

"Study to shew thyself approved unto God, a workman that needeth not to be ashamed, rightly dividing the word of truth. But shun profane and vain babblings: for they will increase unto more ungodliness."

2 Timothy 2:15-16

TITHE HABITUALLY.

❑. Tithe means "tenth." Abraham gave ten percent of his income back to God to show that he honored God as his Provider.

❑ His son Isaac tithed also and reaped one hundredfold the same year he sowed. God rewarded his Seed.

❑ Think like a sower. Your Seed is anything you give to God. Your Harvest is anything He gives back to you. *Habitual sowing guarantees habitual reaping.*

WISDOM WORDS

"Bring ye all the tithes into the storehouse, that there may be meat in Mine house, and prove Me now herewith, saith the Lord of hosts, if I will not open you the windows of heaven, and pour you out a blessing, that there shall not be room enough to receive it."   Malachi 3:10

"Upon the first day of the week let every one of you lay by him in store, as God hath prospered him"
                                                    1 Corinthians 16:2

DEVELOP THE INFORMATION HABIT.

☐ *Readers are Leaders.* Keep up with current events. Daily. Listen. Watch. Observe.

☐ Ask questions. Analyze what happens around you. Open your eyes. Become aware. *Make it a habit.*

☐ *Ignorance creates crisis.* Information solves it.

WISDOM WORDS

"My people are destroyed for lack of knowledge: because thou hast rejected knowledge, I will also reject thee"
Hosea 4:6

"…But through knowledge shall the just be delivered."
Proverbs 11:9

PRACTICE POWER-TALK.

☐ *Power-Talk* is simply *speaking words that produce a desired result in yourself or others.*

☐ Champions *talk* differently. They discuss their future, not their past; their victories, not their defeats. *Never say anything you don't want another to believe.* Start saying what God says about your life.

☐ Words create pictures in your mind. Those pictures decide what you believe. *What you look at the longest will affect you the most.*

WISDOM WORDS

"Death and life are in the power of the tongue: and they that love it shall eat the fruit thereof."

Proverbs 18:21

AVOID ANYONE WHO BREAKS YOUR FOCUS.

❏ *The only reason men fail is broken focus.* It happened with Samson and Delilah. It happened with David and Bathsheba. Don't let it happen to you.

❏ Satan dreads your total concentration on God's Assignment in your life.

❏ *When satan wants to destroy you, he sends a person into your life.*

WISDOM WORDS

"Be not deceived: evil communications corrupt good manners." 1 Corinthians 15:33

"For the Lord giveth wisdom…to deliver thee from the way of the evil man…to deliver thee from the strange woman." Proverbs 2:6,12,16

GET ENOUGH SLEEP.

☐ *When fatigue walks in, faith walks out.*

☐ When you are tired, you change. You *talk* differently, you *think* differently, you assess life differently. And *always inaccurately.*

☐ Accept your personal and unique sleep requirements. Make a habit of going to bed every night at the same time. Your life depends on it.

WISDOM WORDS

"And He said unto them, Come ye yourselves apart into a desert place, and rest a while: for there were many coming and going, and they had no leisure so much as to eat." Mark 6:31

SET A SPECIFIC PRAYER TIME.

❑ Setting a specific prayer time is one of the great secrets in the lives of prayer champions.

❑ Build your daily agenda around your specific prayer time. *Morning* is usually best. Make it the *priority* of the day.

❑ You will be amazed at the power of keeping a *daily appointment* with God.

WISDOM WORDS

"My voice shalt Thou hear in the morning, O Lord; in the morning will I direct my prayer unto Thee, and will look up." Psalm 5:3

LINK TWO GREAT HABITS TOGETHER.

❏ One author dictates his books on a microcassette recorder…while he does his daily five mile walk. *He links two great habits.*

❏ Some keep an Idea Notebook handy during their prayer time. This enables them to easily document ideas fresh from God.

❏ You can do the same. Build on the good habits you already have.

WISDOM WORDS

"For precept must be upon precept, precept upon precept; line upon line, line upon line; here a little, and there a little:"   Isaiah 28:10

MOVE TOWARD ORDER.

❏ Order is the *"accurate arrangement of things."* Develop a passion for it.

❏ You do not park your car in your bedroom. You do not sleep on your kitchen table. You hang your clothes in your closet. You brush your teeth at the bathroom sink. *Order is doing the right thing...at the right time...in the right place.*

❏ *Order increases productivity.* Your productivity increases your contribution. Your contribution increases the rewards you receive in life.

WISDOM WORDS

"And God saw every thing that He had made, and, behold, it was very good. And the evening and the morning were the sixth day. Thus the heavens and the earth were finished, and all the host of them. And on the seventh day God ended His work which He had made"   Genesis 1:31, 2:1-2

PRACTICE THE E.H.A.H. SYSTEM.

❑ *Everything Has A Home.* Your car belongs in the garage. Your dirty clothes belong in the hamper. Everything around you should have an assigned place.

❑ *Everything Has A Home.* Insist on it. Make certain everything is returned to its assigned place.

❑ *Everything Has A Home.* This explains the incredible secret of order. It is the secret of great productivity.

—— *WISDOM WORDS* ——

"Let all things be done decently and in order."
1 Corinthians 14:40

"To every thing there is a season, and a time to every purpose under the heaven:" Ecclesiastes 3:1

RECOGNIZE THE LAW OF EVENTUALITY.

❑ If you smoke three packs of cigarettes a day, what is the *inevitable eventuality?* If you eat two slices of pecan pie late every night, what is the *inevitable eventuality?*

❑ This is the *difference* between champions and losers. *Losers* make decisions that create their desired *present.* *Champions* make decisions that create their desired *future.*

❑ *Your daily habits are carving out an irreversible future.* Are you heading toward what you really want?

WISDOM WORDS

"Be not deceived; God is not mocked: for whatsoever a man soweth, that shall he also reap."

Galatians 6:7

SOW FROM EVERY PAYCHECK.

❑ You want to *receive regularly… sow* regularly. Start the habit of giving something to the work of God out of *every paycheck* you receive. When you sow *consistently*, you will reap *consistently*.

❑ Expect God to multiply your Seed one hundredfold as He promised clearly in Mark 10:30. He *will provide Seed to anyone willing to sow it.*

WISDOM WORDS

"Now He that ministereth seed to the sower both minister bread for your food, and multiply your seed sown, and increase the fruits of your righteousness;"
2 Corinthians 9:10

"While the earth remaineth, seedtime and harvest… shall not cease." Genesis 8:22

DECIDE YOUR DESTINATION.

- ❑ What you are doing *today is creating a permanent* you.

- ❑ *Your habits are vehicles…*taking you into a desirable or undesirable future. Where will your present habits take you in 12 months? In 10 years?

- ❑ *Where will you eventually be if you do not change the direction you are going?* Will you require a tragedy to initiate a change?

WISDOM WORDS

"I call heaven and earth to record this day against you, that I have set before you life and death, blessing and cursing: therefore choose life, that both thou and thy seed may live:"   Deuteronomy 30:19

"Be not deceived; God is not mocked: for whatsoever a man soweth, that shall he also reap."   Galatians 6:7

ESTABLISH GOOD FAMILY HABITS.

❑ Suzanne Wesley had seventeen children. She habitually set aside the first day of each month to devote total attention to her oldest child. Day two was spent with her second child, and so forth. This may explain the greatness of her son, John Wesley.

❑ *Great families usually have great habits.* Follow daily and weekly habits that will create the family unit you desire.

❑ *Designate one night a week as family night.* Cherish it. Build your weekly agenda around it.

—— *WISDOM WORDS* ——

"And if it seem evil unto you to serve the Lord, choose you this day whom ye will serve...but as for me and my house, we will serve the Lord."   Joshua 24:15

MOVE TOWARD EXTRAORDINARY PEOPLE.

- ❏ *Make a habit of pursuing Greatness.*

- ❏ Elisha received a double-portion of God's power because He was willing to pay any price to *stay in the presence* of Elijah, the great prophet.

- ❏ Joshua observed Moses. Ruth reached for Boaz. *You will never possess what you are unwilling to pursue.*

WISDOM WORDS

"He that walketh with wise men shall be wise: but a companion of fools shall be destroyed."

Proverbs 13:20

REMEMBER...
SUCCESS IS A DAILY
EVENT.

❑ *Success is a daily event*...called *joy*. It happens *hourly* when you do the Will of God.

❑ *Habit* is also a daily thing. *Nothing will ever dominate your life unless it happens daily.*

❑ *Focus* on *today's* priorities. *A priority is anything God has commanded you to do today.*

WISDOM WORDS

"It is of the Lord's mercies that we are not consumed, because His compassions fail not. They are new every morning: great is Thy faithfulness."

Lamentations 3:22,23

WELCOME WARFARE.

- ❑ *Warfare is any opposition you experience while pursuing your dreams and goals.* Warfare always surrounds the birth of any miracle.

- ❑ *Opposition is merely a signal that you are making progress.* Hell has noticed, and reacted.

- ❑ A wrathful person who rises up to destroy you is the first clue that satan has targeted you. Welcome it. Heaven must be planning your promotion. Herod sought to kill Jesus. Pharaoh sought to kill Moses. *Satan only attacks those who are next in line for promotion.*

WISDOM WORDS

"Blessed are ye, when men shall revile you, and persecute you, and shall say all manner of evil against you falsely, for My sake. Rejoice, and be exceeding glad: for great is your reward in heaven: for so persecuted they the prophets which were before you."

Matthew 5:11-12

NAME YOUR REAL ENEMY.

❏ You really have one major Enemy in Life—satan.

❏ Don't waste your energy, time and mind on fighting *people*, even though some are being used as *instruments* of satan.

❏ Jesus is The Lion of Judah. Satan is no match. He simply walks around "As a roaring lion."

WISDOM WORDS

"Be sober, be vigilant; because your adversary the devil, as a roaring lion, walketh about, seeking whom he may devour:"   1 Peter 5:8

FIGHT BACK.

☐ During the battles of life, you will be tempted to withdraw, become timid and passive. DON'T.

☐ Satan is a bully. Bullies delight in shy, timid nonfighters. *Real Fighters* intimidate satan.

☐ Whatever satan confronts you with today, be bold. Fight back. *He will Flee.*

WISDOM WORDS

"Resist the devil, and he will flee from you."

James 4:7

USE SPIRITUAL WEAPONS.

❑ Your spiritual weapons are your most powerful weapons in your war against spiritual darkness.

❑ These weapons include praying in the Spirit, speaking the Name of Jesus and quoting the Word. Jesus did it while being tempted by satan in Matthew 4.

❑ Don't forget...satan dreads your discovery of this truth. Remember, nobody else can use these weapons for you.

WISDOM WORDS

"For the weapons of our warfare are not carnal, but mighty through God to the pulling down of strong holds;"
2 Corinthians 10:4

SPEAK THE NAME OF JESUS BOLDLY.

❑ Satan is an ex-employer of God. He and his legions of demons (fallen angels) know the Name of Jesus well.

❑ According to the Word, Jesus is our elder brother, seated at the right hand of the Father, making intercession for us.

❑ Speak His Name today. Boldly. Decisively. Expectantly. Demons tremble at His NAME.

WISDOM WORDS

"That at the name of Jesus every knee should bow, of things in heaven, and things in earth, and things under the earth;"   Philippians 2:10

EXPECT TO WIN.

❑ Someone has said, "Attitude determines Altitude."

❑ Get your attitude right and everything else will fall into place. *Never say anything you don't want satan to believe.*

❑ *Use faith-talk today.* Expect to conquer and master any obstacle you face today. *Jesus makes the difference.*

WISDOM WORDS

"Nay, in all these things we are more than conquerors through him that loved us."   Romans 8:37

REMEMBER THAT PAIN PASSES.

❑ Pain is *discomfort created by disorder.* In your body, in your life relationships, in your finances, or anywhere in your life.

❑ Every Champion has discovered that pain is seasonal. It will pass. *It is the passage to promotion.*

❑ So, don't be discouraged today. Midnight is almost over. A new day is about to dawn in your life.

WISDOM WORDS

"Weeping may endure for a night, but joy cometh in the morning." Psalm 30:5

EXPECT SUPERNATURAL INTERVENTION.

❑ Every artist knows his portrait. Every composer has studied his song.

❑ God, your Creator, has carefully observed each satanic attack against your life.

❑ He will get involved. It is inevitable. And, like Job, when this is over, you will receive a double-portion of His blessings.

WISDOM WORDS

"Ye shall not fear them: for the Lord your God He shall fight for you." Deuteronomy 3:22

"Also the Lord gave Job twice as much as he had before." Job 42:10

KEEP YOUR EYES ON THE SPOILS OF WAR.

❑ *Men fight for a reason — to gain something they want.* On earth, *birth* often decides your rank. But, in the Kingdom of God, *battle decides your rank.*

❑ When David faced Goliath, he was fully aware of the wonderful benefits King Saul offered. When Jesus went to Calvary, He was fully aware of the resurrection — "the joy that was set before Him."

❑ *Keep focused.* The spoils of war are worth your battles.

— *WISDOM WORDS* —

"And it shall be that the man who killeth him (Goliath), the King will enrich him with great riches, and will give him his daughter, and make his father's house free in Israel."   1 Samuel 17:25

"Who for the joy that was set before him endured the cross"   Hebrews 12:2

GIVE GOD TIME TO WORK.

❑ Sometimes those things you desire the most may take longer to achieve. It takes longer to make a Rolls Royce automobile than a bicycle.

❑ Millions of Miracles have been dashed on the Rocks of Impatience. Give God time.

❑ *Something good is happening that you do not see.* Wait joyfully with great expectations.

WISDOM WORDS

"And let us not be weary in well doing: for in due season we shall reap, if we faint not."   Galatians 6:9

INTIMIDATE YOUR INTIMIDATOR.

☐ Your adversary, satan, is really a deceiver and intimidator. He "huffs and blows," lies but *KNOWS"* …that "greater is He that is in you than he that is in the world."

☐ Confront satan. Bind him, "In the Name of Jesus." You have been given authority over satan.

☐ Wear the Mantle of a conqueror today. Fear nothing.

WISDOM WORDS

"For God hath not given us the spirit of fear; but of power, and of love, and of a sound mind."

2 Timothy 1:7

FEED YOUR FAITH.

- ❑ Faith is simply *your confidence in God.* It is energy. It is movement. It is your link to the power of God.

- ❑ *Faith comes when you hear God talk.* Through the Holy Spirit, through the pages of the Bible, or when you hear a man of God speak.

- ❑ Little faith. Great faith. Enduring faith. Whatever. It is like a spiritual muscle. When used properly and often, it becomes an unstoppable force.

WISDOM WORDS

"So then faith cometh by hearing, and hearing by the word of God."   Romans 10:17

"But ye, beloved, building up yourselves on your most holy faith, praying in the Holy Ghost,"   Jude 1:20

REMEMBER THAT MIRACLES BEGIN IN YOUR MOUTH.

❑ *Your enemy reacts to your words.*

❑ *Your enemy will believe whatever you tell him.* Feed faith-words into his ears and he will be demoralized. Talk like a victim and he will be encouraged to attack you again.

❑ Let your words create the current that sweeps you into the heart of God.

WISDOM WORDS

"Death and life are in the power of the tongue: and they that love it shall eat the fruit thereof."

Proverbs 18:21

"For by thy words thou shalt be justified, and by thy words thou shalt be condemned." Matthew 12:37

AIM YOUR SEED LIKE A WEAPON.

❑ Many are beginning to grasp the impact an offering has on the heart of God.

❑ Your offering is a Seed. It is a Signal. It is a Message. It telegraphs your opinion…your hopes…your love for God.

❑ Your Seed-faith offering is also a Weapon. David knew this. When 70,000 men died in 72 hours, he aimed his offering to stop the plague. It worked THEN. It will work NOW.

—— *WISDOM WORDS* ——

"And David built there an altar unto the Lord, and offered burnt offerings and peace offerings. So the Lord was intreated for the land, and the plague was stayed from Israel."   2 Samuel 24:25

"Bring ye all the tithes into the storehouse…and I will rebuke the devourer for your sakes."   Malachi 3:10-11

INFORM AN INTERCESSOR.

❏ Most of us want to fight our battles alone. This is one of the biggest mistakes you could ever make.

❏ *Isolation is the first step toward devastation.* Two are better than one. You need a prayer partner.

❏ Dare to reach. Someone aches to give as badly as you need to receive.

WISDOM WORDS

"If two of you shall agree on earth as touching any thing that they shall ask, it shall be done for them of My Father which is in heaven."   Matthew 18:19

FOCUS ON FASTING.

❏ Fasting is simply abstaining from food for a set period of time. One day, three days, seven days or whatever God speaks to your heart.

❏ Choose your fast wisely. Do it under the instruction of the Holy Spirit, a proven spiritual leader, and I strongly suggest, under the supervision of a physician as well.

❏ *Fasting often bring results when nothing else will.* It could very well be the Master Key that turns the tide in your battle.

WISDOM WORDS

"Is not this the fast that I have chosen? to loose the bands of wickedness, to undo the heavy burdens, and to let the oppressed go free, and that ye break every yoke?"
Isaiah 58:6

LISTEN TO ANOINTED MUSIC.

❑ *Godly music drives evil spirits away.*

❑ When depression enters, and the battle rages... turn on a music cassette that ushers in the Presence of God. Satan reacts to it. He fears it.

❑ *Create the climate that unlocks the best in you.* Listen to music that glorifies your Heavenly Father.

WISDOM WORDS

"And it came to pass, when the evil spirit from God was upon Saul, that David took an harp, and played with his hand: so Saul was refreshed, and was well, and the evil spirit departed from him."   1 Samuel 16:23

BECOME A MASTER WARRIOR.

☐ Fighting is a *learned* art.

☐ Sit at the feet of the Holy Spirit. Permit His Mentorship. Take time to learn His battle-techniques.

☐ Remember, *you will never OUTGROW warfare. You simply must learn to fight.*

WISDOM WORDS

"Blessed be the Lord my strength, which teacheth my hands to war, and my fingers to fight:"   Psalm 144:1

SEE YOUR BATTLE AS A GATE TO PROMOTION.

❑ Warfare may appear to be an obstacle to you. However, God will use it to determine your next promotion.

❑ Daniel was promoted...*after* the lions den. Job received a double blessing...after his suffering. Joseph reached the palace...*after* the pit and the prison.

❑ Don't run from the battle. Stay around for your crown. Award ceremony is the next scheduled event.

WISDOM WORDS

"Blessed is the man that endureth temptation: for when he is tried, he shall receive the crown of life, which the Lord hath promised to them that love Him."

James 1:12

PUT ON YOUR SPIRITUAL ARMOR.

❑ As you pray today, mentally visualize yourself putting on the whole armor of God around you.

❑ Pull down the Helmet of Salvation to protect your mind. Wrap Truth around your body. Take the breastplate of Righteousness.

❑ Put the Gospel of Peace on your feet. Grasp the Sword of the Spirit, and the Shield of Faith. Now ...SEIZE THE DAY.

— WISDOM WORDS —

"Put on the whole armour of God, that ye may be able to stand against the wiles of the devil."

Ephesians 6:11

REFUSE THE WHIRLPOOL OF WORRY.

❏ *Worry is meditation on things that torment you.* It is sin.

❏ *Worry is spoken or unspoken fears.* You can stop it by meditating on the Word of God instead.

❏ Worry kept the Israelites out of the Promised Land. Refuse to let it destroy you.

WISDOM WORDS

"Though I walk in the midst of trouble, Thou wilt revive me: Thou shalt stretch forth Thine hand against the wrath of mine enemies, and Thy right hand shall save me."   Psalm 138:7

PINPOINT PROBLEM PEOPLE.

❑ People are different. Some are champions. Some are losers. Some unite. Some divide. You will always have two kinds of friends: those who make *deposits* and those who make *withdrawals*.

❑ Your warfare will reveal the true character of those around you.

❑ Do not be deceived. Avoid those who do not display the nature of Christ. *The worth of any friendship can be measured by its contribution to your victories.*

WISDOM WORDS

"Now I beseech you, brethren, mark them which cause divisions and offences contrary to the doctrine which ye have learned; and avoid them. For they that are such serve not our Lord Jesus Christ, but their own belly; and by good words and fair speeches deceive the hearts of the simple." Romans 16:17-18

NEVER FIGHT HALF-HEARTEDLY.

❑ A divided *country* falls. A divided *home* deteriorates. A divided *mind* becomes powerless.

❑ *Your battle deserves your full attention.* Winning it authorizes God to promote you.

❑ Satan is dead serious about destroying you. It is high time you become serious about *winning*.

WISDOM WORDS

"Whatsoever thy hand findeth to do, do it with thy might;"   Ecclesiastes 9:10

HARNESS YOUR MIND.

- ❏ You must make your mind your *servant*. You must tell it what to do, what you think about and what you meditate upon. *Boss it*.

- ❏ Some believe that your heart is actually your subconscious mind…where you store your thoughts. So, fill up your Mental Warehouse with the Word of God.

- ❏ *What happens in your mind is likely to happen in your future.* Meditate on specific scriptures today that unlock your faith in God.

WISDOM WORDS

"Finally, brethren, whatsoever things are true, whatsoever things are honest, whatsoever things are just, whatsoever things are pure, whatsoever things are lovely, whatsoever things are of good report; if there be any virtue, and if there be any praise, think on these things."   Philippians 4:8

LEARN TO LAUGH.

❑ *Find something that makes you laugh today.*

❑ *Laugh often.* Make a conscious effort to release your joy in this way.

❑ Physicians report that laughter actually *accelerates* the healing process when your body is sick.

WISDOM WORDS

"A merry heart doeth good like a medicine: but a broken spirit drieth the bones." Proverbs 17:22

REFUSE TO PANIC.

❑ Your battles appear suddenly, without forewarning.

❑ *Your biggest mistakes will happen during the first few moments of a satanic attack.* Surprise is his strategy.

❑ *Don't Panic.* Be still. Stop and listen carefully to the inner voice of the Holy Spirit. Time is your friend. Wait for the answer. *Patience is the weapon that forces deception to reveal itself.*

—— *WISDOM WORDS* ——

"Ye shall not need to fight in this battle: set yourselves, stand ye still, and see the salvation of the Lord with you, O Judah and Jerusalem: fear not, nor be dismayed; to morrow go out against them: for the Lord will be with you." 2 Chronicles 20:17

STAY FOCUSED.

❏ *The secret of every failure is broken focus.* The secret of every success is total focus.

❏ You cannot meditate on your past and your future at the same time. So, focus on your desired future.

❏ *Be ruthless with distractions.* Remember, *creativity* is the *search* for alternatives. *Concentration* is the *elimination* of them.

WISDOM WORDS

"Brethren, I count not myself to have apprehended: but this one thing I do, forgetting those things which are behind, and reaching forth unto those things which are before, I press toward the mark for the prize of the high calling of God in Christ Jesus."   Philippians 3:13-14

CONSULT YOUR MENTOR.

❑ *A mentor is someone you have chosen to teach you.*

❑ Your mentor can be either a bottleneck or a bridge to your dream. He can create strife or stimulate. Consult the mentor most likely *to build your faith.*

❑ Moses was a mentor of Joshua. Paul was a mentor to Timothy. Elijah was a mentor to Elisha. *Warfare is the ideal time to reach for YOUR mentor.* Two are better than one.

WISDOM WORDS

"A wise man is strong; yea, a man of knowledge increaseth strength. For by wise counsel thou shalt make thy war: and in multitude of counsellors there is safety."   Proverbs 24:5-6

SEE THE BIG PICTURE.

❑ The Apostle Paul was not afraid to suffer. He knew that those who *suffer* will eventually *reign* with Christ.

❑ *The Big Picture...is seeing the future reward for present endurance.* Losers make decisions that create a desired present. But champions make decisions that will create *a desired future*.

❑ Battles are simply birth-plans that accompany the birth of every great dream.

WISDOM WORDS

"For our light affliction, which is but for a moment, worketh for us a far more exceeding and eternal weight of glory;"   2 Corinthians 4:17

CALL ON YOUR GREATEST GIFTS.

❑ *You have something that someone else needs.* God gave it to you. Find it and use it.

❑ David was good with a slingshot. Goliath was simply a signal to use the gift. What do you do *well? The season of war is the time to do it.*

❑ *Whatever you have been given is capable of creating anything else God has promised you.*

WISDOM WORDS

"Wherefore I put thee in remembrance that thou stir up the gift of God, which is in thee by the putting on of my hands."   2 Timothy 1:6

PRAY IN THE HOLY GHOST.

❑ Some people learn to sing. Some people learn public speaking. Others do not. Some Christians learn how to pray. Others do not.

❑ *Praying in the Holy Ghost is worth learning.*

❑ *Use your prayer language today.* Release the Holy Spirit to talk to the Father for you. *It will turn the tide of battle.*

WISDOM WORDS

"But ye, beloved, building up yourselves on your most holy faith, praying in the Holy Ghost,"   Jude 1:20

STUDY OBEDIENCE.

❑ Obedience is simple doing exactly what God instructs. It will require discipline, total focus and determination.

❑ Obedience is the only thing God has ever required of man. That's why your smallest act of obedience is documented and celebrated by God.

❑ Anything you give *attention* to, you will do well. So, find what makes God happy…and do it.

WISDOM WORDS

"Study to shew thyself approved unto God, a workman that needeth not to be ashamed, rightly dividing the word of truth."   2 Timothy 2:15

REMEMBER, OBEDIENCE BEGINS AT WAKE-UP.

❑ Begin this day with prayer. Ask yourself. "Is my schedule for today truly the agenda God has chosen for me?" If not, *change it.*

❑ Yesterday is in the *tomb.* Tomorrow is in the *womb.* The most important day of your life is *today.*

❑ Concentrate on walking in total obedience for the next 24 hours. Keep your ear next to the mouth of God *every single hour.*

WISDOM WORDS

"My voice shalt Thou hear in the morning, O Lord; in the morning will I direct my prayer unto Thee, and will look up." Psalm 5:3

GET TO KNOW GOD'S VOICE.

❑ God talks…more than anyone you will ever meet. He talks as often *as you need help.*

❑ I cannot explain to you my mother's voice. You would have to spend time with my mother.

❑ I cannot explain to you my Heavenly Father's voice. You will have to spend time with Him to know His *voice. Obedience is impossible unless you discern His voice.*

WISDOM WORDS

"My sheep hear My voice, and I know them, and they follow Me:"   John 10:27

SCHEDULE INTIMATE MOMENTS WITH GOD.

❑ You make appointments with your doctor, your lawyer, your boss. Why not schedule a one-hour appointment daily with God?

❑ Do it every day *at the same time.* This helps create rhythm in your life.

❑ *You* will *hear* what you have never heard before. You will *discover* what you have never known before. You will *become* what you have always wanted to become.

WISDOM WORDS

"He went into his house; and his windows being open in his chamber toward Jerusalem, he kneeled upon his knees three times a day, and prayed, and gave thanks before his God, as he did aforetime."   Daniel 6:10

RECOGNIZE MESSENGERS FROM GOD.

❑ When satan wants to *destroy* you, he sends a *person*. When God wants to *bless you*, He sends a *person*.

❑ *Recognize them.* Whether they are packaged like a John the Baptist in a loincloth of camel's hair, or the silk robes of King Solomon.

❑ Your reaction to a man or woman of God is carefully documented by God. When God talks to you, it is often through the spiritual leaders in your life. *Don't ignore them.*

WISDOM WORDS

"He that receiveth a prophet in the name of a prophet shall receive a prophet's reward; and he that receiveth a righteous man in the name of a righteous man shall receive a righteous man's reward."   Matthew 10:41

FACE YOUR SINS HONESTLY.

❑ Everyone has sinned against God. Publicly or privately.

❑ You are instructed in the Word to confess that sin and turn away from it. Do it now. *Obey Him.*

❑ Only a fool would attempt to deceive God. Your confession will unlock His mercy.

WISDOM WORDS

"He that covereth his sins shall not prosper: but whoso confesseth and forsaketh them shall have mercy."

Proverbs 28:13

RUN TOWARD GOD.

❑ *Things happen in the presence of God that do not happen anywhere else.*

❑ When you get in His presence, you *think* differently. You *talk* differently. You *act* differently. Your *best* comes out of you.

❑ So get started today. Like any damaged product, we must *return* to our manufacturer for repair.

WISDOM WORDS

"All that the Father giveth me shall come to me; and him that cometh to me I will in no wise cast out."

John 6:37

OBEY YOUR PARENTS.

❑ *Your reaction toward your parents influences God's reaction towards you.*

❑ In the Ten Commandments, the commandment to honor your parents was the first to be followed by a promise.

❑ Carefully consider any advice your parents give you. *Honor* it. Contribute to their life. Take their opinions seriously. It will be forever written on the mind of God.

WISDOM WORDS

"Children, obey your parents in the Lord: for this is right." Ephesians 6:1

OBEY YOUR BOSS.

❑ Bosses are not always easy to please. They may sometimes be like sandpaper God is using to polish the rough edges of your life.

❑ It is awesome that the Creator of this universe stopped long enough to personally advise *employees*…to be obedient to their *employers*.

❑ Obedience in the workplace consists of *careful listening, taking notes and total concentration on completion of a task*. Do it. God will prosper you for it.

WISDOM WORDS

"Servants, be obedient to them that are your masters according to the flesh, with fear and trembling, in singleness of your heart, as unto Christ;"

Ephesians 6:5

LEARN TO LISTEN.

❏ *Somebody knows something you do not know.* That information may be invaluable. You have to *listen* to receive it.

❏ Something inside you may want to scream out for attention. You have to be heard. Restrain yourself. *Learn to listen.*

❏ Remember, God talks. How often? *As often as you need help.*

WISDOM WORDS

"A wise man will hear, and will increase learning; and a man of understanding shall attain unto wise counsels:"
Proverbs 1:5

DESPISE DIOBEDIENCE.

❑ You must develop a hatred for evil. *You can only conquer what you hate*.

❑ Take a moment to note that millions of babies are murdered by *abortion*. Thousands have splattered their blood on our highways because of *alcoholism*. Thousands more are destroyed through *drugs*. All of these are *results of disobedience*.

❑ Determine to obey. *Walk toward God*. Toward righteousness. You will never regret it.

WISDOM WORDS

"The fear of the Lord is to hate evil."   Proverbs 8:13

FEAR GOD.

❏ Fearing God is not necessarily being afraid of Him. It means to honor Him and have a healthy respect for His opinions, instructions and plans.

❏ What you respect will *come toward* you. What you do not respect will *move away* from you.

❏ God honors those who fear Him. Attending His house on the Lord's Day, tithing and morning prayer are signals to Him that He matters to you.

WISDOM WORDS

"Let us hear the conclusion of the whole matter: Fear God, and keep His commandments: for this is the whole duty of man. For God shall bring every work into judgment, with every secret thing, whether it be good, or whether it be evil." Ecclesiastes 12:13-14

EXAMINE THE REWARDS OF OBEDIENCE.

❑ Obedience is doing whatever God instructs you to do. Each instruction is linked to a miracle in your future.

❑ Each act of obedience shortens the distance to any miracle you are pursuing.

❑ Remember God only feels obligated to the obedient. The obedient always receive answers to their prayers.

WISDOM WORDS

"And whatsoever we ask, we receive of Him, because we keep His commandments, and do those things that are pleasing in His sight."   1 John 3:22

CONSIDER THE CONSEQUENCES OF YOUR REBELLION.

❏ Rebellion is punished. *Always.* It may not happen today, but it is inevitable. Each Seed of disobedience is like a magnet attracting tragedies into your life.

❏ *God will never advance you beyond your last act of disobedience.* Joshua learned this at the Battles of Ai, when Achan attempted a cover-up of his sin. The Israelites lost the battle.

❏ God is not stupid. He is not blind. He sees everything. Sooner or later…He reacts to it. *You cannot afford the losses your rebellion will create.*

WISDOM WORDS

"Then shall they call upon Me, but I will not answer; they shall seek Me early, but they shall not find Me: For that they hated knowledge, and did not choose the fear of the Lord: Therefore shall they eat of the fruit of their own way, and be filled with their own devices."

Proverbs 1:28,29,31

APPRECIATE ORDER.

❑ Order is *the accurate arrangement of things.* Your car is parked in your garage. Your clothes hang *orderly* in your closet.

❑ When you increase order (the accurate arrangement of people and events) you increase your *productivity*. Plan your day carefully.

❑ Unplanned hours will always gravitate toward your weakness. Unplanned days are unproductive days. *Unplanned days are incubators for your greatest mistakes.*

WISDOM WORDS

"Let all things be done decently and in order."
1 Corinthians 14:40

PRAY OVER EVERY DECISION.

❏ *Something happens when you pray that would not have happened had you not prayed.*

❏ Every decision you make is a turning point in your life. Making the right decision determines whether you succeed or fail.

❏ Prayer is the proof you respect God. It is a sign that you recognize His power to change your circumstances. It attracts God. *Do it.*

WISDOM WORDS

"...The effectual fervent prayer of a righteous man availeth much."   James 5:16

HONOR THE CHAIN OF AUTHORITY.

❑ Imagine a nation without a leader. A workplace without a boss. An army without a general. *Authority creates order.*

❑ God created the chain of authority. The pastor that *oversees* his congregation. The father that *rules* his home. The employer who *supervises* his staff.

❑ *Honor the chain of authority in your life.* Joseph did. David did. It is the *hidden secret* to promotion.

WISDOM WORDS

"Obey them that have the rule over you, and submit yourselves:"   Hebrews 13:17

EXPECT BLESSINGS.

❑ You have listened. You have heard. You have obeyed the instructions of God. Now, *expect miracles.*

❑ Blessings are benefits from God that increase your joy, and enable you to complete His instructions for your life. They are promised only to the *obedient.*

❑ Obedience is *always* rewarded. Blessings are guaranteed to "those who walk uprightly." *Obedience is the only real proof of your faith in God.*

— WISDOM WORDS —

"And all these blessings shall come on thee, and overtake thee, if thou shalt hearken unto the voice of the Lord thy God."   Deuteronomy 28:2

"For the Lord God is a sun and shield: the Lord will give grace and glory: no good thing will He withhold from them that walk uprightly."   Psalm 84:11

PLAN ON SUPERNATURAL PROTECTION.

❏ Every day of your life, satan will make attempts to destroy you. The story of Job illustrates this.

❏ You are not capable of totally protecting yourself. You will require *supernatural* interventions.

❏ Plan on supernatural protection *daily*. It is one of your rewards for hourly *obedience*.

WISDOM WORDS

"But if thou shalt indeed obey His voice, and do all that I speak; then I will be an enemy unto thine enemies, and an adversary unto thine adversaries."

Exodus 23:22

COMMAND SICKNESS TO LEAVE.

- ❑ God wants you well. He wants you healthy in your body, mind and spirit.

- ❑ In the Old Testament, He gave Israel dietary laws regarding foods they were to avoid. *Disobedience* brought *sickness*. *Obedience* brought *health*.

- ❑ Obey God *today*. Then command sickness and disease to depart from you and your household, in the Name of Jesus.

WISDOM WORDS

"And ye shall serve the Lord your God, and He shall bless thy bread, and thy water; and I will take sickness away from the midst of thee."   Exodus 23:25

LOOK AT LOSERS AND LEARN.

❑ When you see an alcoholic or drug addict, you see someone who has lost the most precious things in life—his health, loving relationships and self-confidence.

❑ God promises *gain* to the obedient. He guarantees loss to the disobedient.

❑ Every loser can be a lesson to us. LEARN.

WISDOM WORDS

"There is a way which seemeth right unto a man, but the end thereof are the ways of death."

Proverbs 14:12

STUDY CHAMPIONS.

❏ David was a champion. Samuel was a champion. *They walked the path of obedience.*

❏ Learn from their mistakes, their successes, their lives. Losers build their lives around their *weaknesses.* Champions build their lives around their *strengths.*

❏ You are destined for greatness, too. *Talk* it. *Believe* it. *Live* it. Champions simply use the *Master Key* of Obedience.

— *WISDOM WORDS* —

"And what shall I more say? for the time would fail me to tell of Gedeon, and of Barak, and of Samson, and of Jephthae; of David also, and Samuel, and of the prophets: Who through faith subdued kingdoms, wrought righteousness, obtained promises, stopped the mouths of lions, Quenched the violence of fire, escaped the edge of the sword, out of weakness were made strong, waxed valiant in fight, turned to flight the armies of the aliens." Hebrews 11:32-34

DISCERN GOD'S DAILY AGENDA.

❑ Your agenda (schedule for today) should be decided in the *presence of God.* Your daily agenda will create miracles or tragedies depending on whether or not you are led by the Spirit of God. HOURLY.

❑ *Obedience is an hourly event.*

❑ Your inner peace is a *signal.* Don't make a phone call, an appointment or a decision *unless you are at peace* in your heart about it.

WISDOM WORDS

"For as many as are led by the Spirit of God, they are the sons of God."   Romans 8:14

ENDURE CORRECTION.

- ❏ *Wisdom begins with correction.* Errors must be exposed. Mistakes must be admitted.

- ❏ Think back over your life. Think of the person who taught you the most. He was probably the one who *corrected* you the most.

- ❏ Hell is full of people who *rejected* correction. Heaven is full of people who *accepted* it.

WISDOM WORDS

"For whom the Lord loveth He chasteneth, and scourgeth every son whom He receiveth. Now no chastening for the present seemeth to be joyous, but grievous: nevertheless afterward it yieldeth the peaceable fruit of righteousness unto them which are exercised thereby."

Hebrews 12:6,11

DEMAND OBEDIENCE FROM YOUR CHILDREN.

❑ Your children are gifts from the Lord. Take time to unlock their greatness. Help create *order* in their lives.

❑ Make a list of their daily chores. They deserve to know your *specific expectations* of them.

❑ *Penalize them* for disobedience. *Reward them* for obedience. Do it consistently. They are worth the time and effort.

WISDOM WORDS

"Chasten thy son while there is hope, and let not thy soul spare for his crying."   Proverbs 19:18

ESCAPE THE CURSE.

❑ Tithe means "tenth." The Bible indicates ten percent of your income belongs to God.

❑ This tithe is "Holy Seed." Each time you receive your paycheck, give ten percent back to God, like a Seed that a farmer sows to create a crop. Then, *expect a Harvest.*

❑ Millions live under a curse. They have hoarded the tithes for themselves. Whatever you do, obey God in your giving. *Escape the curse.*

— *WISDOM WORDS* —

"Will a man rob God? Yet ye have robbed Me. But ye say, Wherein have we robbed Thee? In tithes and offerings. Ye are cursed with a curse: for ye have robbed Me, even this whole nation. Bring ye all the tithes into the storehouse, that there may be meat in Mine house, and prove me now herewith, saith the Lord of hosts, if I will not open you the windows of heaven, and pour you out a blessing, that there shall not be room enough to receive it."
                                                    Malachi 3:8-10

DON'T RUN FROM YOUR CALLING.

❑ You may be called to the Ministry. *Don't fight it.* Thousands rebel every day against the call of God into the ministry, satan wreaks havoc with their life because of it.

❑ Think back. See if you can remember any moment God spoke to your heart to become a pastor, an evangelist, a missionary. *Consider it again.*

❑ *Are you called?* In Jesus Name, find a man of God who will mentor you and unlock this eternal anointing upon your life. You will *never be happy anywhere else.*

— *WISDOM WORDS* —

"And He said unto them, Go ye into all the world, and preach the gospel to every creature."   Mark 16:15

"Before I formed thee in the belly I knew thee; and before thou camest forth out of the womb I sanctified thee, and I ordained thee a prophet unto the nations."
Jeremiah 1:5

DISCERN YOUR ASSIGNMENT.

- ❑ When God created you, He gave you certain gifts and talents *to accomplish something He wanted you to do.* We call that *"an Assignment."*

- ❑ *The problem that infuriates you the most is often the problem God has assigned you to solve.*

- ❑ *Everything God creates is a solution to something.* You are a life-jacket to someone drowning. Find them. *Those who unlock your compassion are those to whom you have been assigned.*

WISDOM WORDS

"I will praise thee; for I am fearfully and wonderfully made: marvellous are Thy works; and that my soul knoweth right well." Psalm 139:14

NEVER STAY WHERE GOD HAS NOT ASSIGNED YOU.

❑ You are *geographically* designed. This means that your nationality, your race, sex and even where you were born was decided by God.

❑ You are *geographically* assigned. This means there is a place, a city, a location where God wants you. *There...is where you will flourish and succeed.*

❑ Elijah was *sent* to the brook. There he was *reassigned* to the widow of Zaraphath. *Each instruction from God is linked to your Assignment.* Your financial provisions are usually *waiting* for you at *the place where God has assigned you.*

WISDOM WORDS

"And the word of the Lord came unto him, saying, Get thee hence, and turn thee eastward, and hide thyself by the brook Cherith...And the word of the Lord came unto him, saying, Arise, get thee to Zarephath, which belongeth to Zidon, and dwell there:"

1 Kings 17:2,3,8,9

DO SOMETHING RIGHT TODAY.

❑ It is easy to impress God. Just do something *right*. Follow His instructions. Those instructions may come through His Word, the inner voice of the Holy Spirit, or through men of God in your life.

❑ Attend church *faithfully*. Tithe *consistently*. Pray *daily*. Read the Bible *habitually*. Witness to someone about Jesus.

❑ Those little golden hinges swing huge doors to miracles. Get started...NOW. Humble yourself. *Reach. You will succeed.*

WISDOM WORDS

"If My people, which are called by My name, shall humble themselves, and pray, and seek My face, and turn from their wicked ways; then will I hear from heaven, and will forgive their sin, and will heal their land."   2 Chronicles 7:14

RETURN FOR REPAIR.

❑ When you receive a product you have ordered through the mail, it may arrive damaged. You have to return it to the manufacturer for repair.

❑ Your life is the same way. Sometimes the painful experiences have left us damaged. Only God can truly repair us.

❑ *Don't be afraid of God.* Dare to reach for Him. He loves you far more than you will ever know.

WISDOM WORDS

"Come now, and let us reason together, saith the Lord: though your sins be as scarlet, they shall be as white as snow; though they be red like crimson, they shall be as wool."   Isaiah 1:18

ANALYZE ADVERSITY.

- ❑ There are four ways to respond to a crisis: *Maximize* it. *Minimize* it. *Advertise* it. *Analyze* it.

- ❑ Maximizing...is to *exaggerate* the crisis. Minimizing....is to *understate* the crisis. Advertising...is to *tell* the whole world about it. Analyzing...is *extracting* useful information from it.

- ❑ *Crisis is merely concentrated information.* Adversity is simply your enemies' reaction to your progress. Taking the time to analyze it will benefit you.

WISDOM WORDS

"In the day of prosperity be joyful, but in the day of adversity consider"   Ecclesiastes 7:14

DON'T PANIC.

❑ Something may happen today that shocks you. Don't worry about it. *God anticipated it.*

❑ Remember, satan is merely an ex-employee of Heaven. God knows him quite well. He *fired* him.

❑ Get alone today in the presence of God. Fear will die and courage will flourish.

WISDOM WORDS

"Be still, and know that I am God"   Psalm 46:10

PURSUE WORTHY COUNSEL.

❑ *Someone knows something you need to know.* Something that can help you survive and even succeed in the most painful chapter of your life.

❑ Ignorance can be deadly. *Don't risk it.*

❑ Whatever you do today, take the time to *listen* to Godly advice. *True champions do.*

WISDOM WORDS

"Where no counsel is, the people fall: but in the multitude of counsellors there is safety."

Proverbs 11:14

TRUST GOD TO STOP THE ATTACK.

❑ You serve a very capable God. He can turn the hearts of kings.

❑ You are on His mind this very moment. Your tears, your pain and fears are very important to Him.

❑ He is about to move. *Trust Him.*

WISDOM WORDS

"He maketh wars to cease"   Psalm 46:9

KEEP THE SPIRIT OF A FINISHER.

❏ Anyone can *begin* a marathon. Champions *finish* them.

❏ Everyone experiences adversity. It is those who stay strong *to the finish* who are rewarded.

❏ *Face yourself.* Determine to "go the distance." Keep aflame the *Spirit of a Finisher.*

WISDOM WORDS

"I have fought a good fight, I have finished my course, I have kept the faith:"   2 Timothy 4:7

FOCUS ON THE BENEFITS OF ENDURANCE.

❑ Every battle is for a *reason*. Every battle is for a *season*. Don't forget it…ENDURE.

❑ When you are tired, exhausted and discouraged. ENDURE.

❑ Endurance is rewarded. Always. *It is the only thing in eternity that will be rewarded.*

WISDOM WORDS

"…But he that endureth to the end shall be saved."
Matthew 10:22

DON'T FEEL ALONE TODAY.

❑ You may feel targeted by hell. Your world may be crashing around you. *Don't feel alone.*

❑ Those closest to you may not show it, but *they are hurting, too.*

❑ So, don't yield to self-pity. *Pity parties merely postpone your victory.* You are not alone.

WISDOM WORDS

"Be sober, be vigilant; because your adversary the devil, as a roaring lion, walketh about, seeking whom he may devour: Whom resist stedfast in the faith, knowing that the same afflictions are accomplished in your brethren that are in the world."   1 Peter 5:8-9

SET THE BIG PICTURE.

❑ *Nothing is ever as it first appears.*

❑ Pain passes. Adversity passes. Look beyond your current hardships. *Something incredible is being produced.*

❑ The resurrection followed the crucifixion. Promotion follows adversity. So get your eyes on the *bigger* picture.

WISDOM WORDS

"For our light affliction, which is but for a moment, worketh for us a far more exceeding and eternal weight of glory;"   2 Corinthians 4:17

GUARD YOUR MIND.

❏ Your mind is the *birthplace*...the *incubator*...the *beginning point* of everything you do.

❏ Satan knows this. His entire strategy is to *break* your focus, *sabotage* your concentration and *abort* your Assignment from God.

❏ So *the real battleground of life is your mind.* Guard it well.

WISDOM WORDS

"Finally, brethren, whatsoever things are true, whatsoever things are honest, whatsoever things are just, whatsoever things are pure, whatsoever things are lovely, whatsoever things are of good report; if there be any virtue, and if there be any praise, think on these things."   Philippians 4:8

REMEMBER SEASONS CHANGE.

❑ *Attacks don't last forever.*

❑ People change. Weather changes. Circumstances change. So don't be discouraged today. *Expect* supernatural and dramatic changes.

❑ Tomorrow is coming. *Your future is unlike any yesterday you have ever known.*

WISDOM WORDS

"…weeping may endure for a night, but joy cometh in the morning." Psalm 30:5

CREATE YOUR PRAYER CIRCLE.

❑ *One cannot multiply.*

❑ Increase begins with two. Jesus promised results from the Prayer of Agreement.

❑ Make a list of seven effective intercessors for your life. Contact them. They are your *Circle of Protection.*

— *WISDOM WORDS* —

"Again I say unto you, That if two of you shall agree on earth as touching any thing that they shall ask, it shall be done for them of My Father which is in heaven. For where two or three are gathered together in My name, there am I in the midst of them."   Matthew 18:19-20

READ THE STORIES OF CHAMPIONS.

❑ People are different. Some are losers. Some are champions. *Study the Champions.*

❑ Meditate on the Biblical accounts of David, Abraham, Joseph, the apostle Paul. Visit your local library. Read the biographies of great men.

❑ Readers become leaders. Read, read, *read.*

WISDOM WORDS

"Who through faith subdued kingdoms, wrought righteousness, obtained promises, stopped the mouths of lions, Quenched the violence of fire, escaped the edge of the sword, out of weakness were made strong, waxed valiant in fight, turned to flight the armies of the aliens."

Hebrews 11:33-34

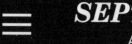

FOCUS ON FASTING.

❑ Adversity is a season of *unusual* attack. So, consider using *unusual weapons.*

❑ Fasting is a *feared weapon* in battle. It is a tool that sharpens your spiritual sensitivity to God.

❑ *Use it.*

WISDOM WORDS

"Is not this the fast that I have chosen? to loose the bands of wickedness, to undo the heavy burdens, and to let the oppressed go free, and that ye break every yoke?"
Isaiah 58:6

REMEMBER THE POWER OF PRAISE.

❑ *Praise is your verbal and physical response to the greatness of God.*

❑ Music...singing...worship...creates an atmosphere for miracles. You are responsible for the climate you permit around you.

❑ *The atmosphere you permit determines the product you produce.*

WISDOM WORDS

"Let the high praises of God be in their mouth, and a twoedged sword in their hand;...to bind their kings with chains...to execute upon them the judgment written: this honour have all His saints. Praise ye the Lord."

Psalm 149:6-9

EXPECT RESCUE.

❑ Adversity is just a page, not your whole book.

❑ *Adversity is simply hell's attempt to abort the next season of blessing God has scheduled for your life.*

❑ The eyes of your Father are upon you. Expect a miraculous rescue.

WISDOM WORDS

"The Lord upholdeth all that fall, and raiseth up all those that be bowed down."   Psalm 145:14

FIND SOMEONE ELSE IN TROUBLE.

❑ *Your wealth is determined by the kinds of problems you are willing to solve for someone.*

❑ Mechanics solve car problems. Lawyers solve legal problems. Doctors solve physical problems.

❑ You are a walking solution to someone in trouble. *Find them.*

WISDOM WORDS

"And if thou draw out thy soul to the hungry, and satisfy the afflicted soul; then shall thy light rise in obscurity, and thy darkness be as the noon day: And the Lord shall guide thee continually, and satisfy thy soul in drought, and make fat thy bones: and thou shalt be like a watered garden, and like a spring of water, whose waters fail not."   Isaiah 58:10-11

AVOID VICTIM MENTALITY.

❑ *Any wounded animal attracts attack.*

❑ *Weakness is an invitation to bullies.* So don't talk nor think like a victim of your circumstances.

❑ You are more than a conqueror. *Act* like it. *Talk* like it. The love of God is keeping you today.

WISDOM WORDS

"Who shall separate us from the love of Christ? shall tribulation, or distress, or persecution, or famine, or nakedness, or peril, or sword? Nay, in all these things we are more than conquerors through Him that loved us."   Romans 8:35,37

TRUST GOD.
LOVE PEOPLE.

❑ God never commanded you to trust people.

❑ God commanded you to *love* people and *trust Him*.

❑ *Know the difference.* Your joy and victory depend on it.

WISDOM WORDS

"It is better to trust in the Lord than to put confidence in man."   Psalm 118:8

MARK YOUR ENEMY.

- ❑ When satan launches a strike against you, it is usually through a *person*.

- ❑ Your enemy is *anyone who attempts to stop the will of God from being fulfilled in your life.*

- ❑ Identify and avoid anyone who breaks your focus through stirring up strife and division.

WISDOM WORDS

"Now I beseech you, brethren, mark them which cause divisions and offences contrary to the doctrine which ye have learned; and avoid them."   Romans 16:17

PURIFY YOURSELF BEFORE GOD.

❑ You are the offspring of a Holy God. This explains your insatiable appetite to live a holy and pure life.

❑ Sin happens. *Just don't cover it up.* Bring it to God.

❑ Repentance is the golden hinge that opens the door to the next season of your life.

WISDOM WORDS

"Behold, the Lord's hand is not shortened, that it cannot save; neither His ear heavy, that it cannot hear: But your iniquities have separated between you and your God, and your sins have hid His face from you, that He will not hear."   Isaiah 59:1-2

SOAK YOURSELF IN THE SCRIPTURES.

- ❑ Your mind is like soil. It will grow *any Seed* you sow into it, *good or bad.*

- ❑ When you sow *words spoken by God* into your mind, you are sowing energy, life, light and hope *into yourself.*

- ❑ His Word is like a spiritual vaccination that strips satan of his power against your life.

WISDOM WORDS

"Unless Thy law had been my delights, I should then have perished in mine affliction." Psalm 119:92

"The law of his God is in his heart; none of his steps shall slide." Psalm 37:31

SEPTEMBER 22
ADVERSITY

REMEMBER WHO IS WITH YOU.

❑ *Two are better than one.* God said it. Believe it.

❑ You are never, never, *never* alone in this world.

❑ Invisible, but undeniable, your Creator is standing beside you this very moment, even as you are reading these very words.

WISDOM WORDS

"...for He hath said, I will never leave thee, nor forsake thee. So that we may boldly say, The Lord is my helper, and I will not fear what man shall do unto me."

Hebrews 13:5-6

KEEP WALKING.

❑ Picture this. You are in your car. You are driving in a heavy hailstorm. You don't stop...but keep driving knowing you will *move out of the storm's range.*

❑ Remember Joseph. Remember David. Every day of adversity was simply a *stepping stone toward the throne.*

❑ *Keep walking.*

— WISDOM WORDS —

"When thou passest through the waters, I will be with thee; and through the rivers, they shall not overflow thee: when thou walkest through the fire, thou shalt not be burned; neither shall the flame kindle upon thee. For I am the Lord thy God"   Isaiah 43:2-3

NEVER, NEVER, NEVER GIVE UP.

❏ Your dreams and goals are worth any fight, any waiting, any price. *Don't give up.*

❏ Your perseverance demoralizes your enemy. Don't give up.

❏ Patience is a weapon. *Don't give up.*

WISDOM WORDS

"And Jesus said unto him, No man, having put his hand to the plough, and looking back, is fit for the kingdom of God."   Luke 9:62

LOOK FOR DOUBLE-BLESSING

❑ Read carefully the accounts of Job, Joseph, Daniel and others. Their adversity always birthed a season of Double-Portion Blessings in their lives.

❑ They discovered that *false accusation is often the last stage before supernatural promotion.*

❑ So look for Double-Blessing. *Miracles are coming towards you…or going past you every day.* Recognize them.

— WISDOM WORDS —

"And the Lord turned the captivity of Job, when he prayed for his friends: also the Lord gave Job twice as much as he had before."   Job 42:10

BE TOUGH.

- ❏ *Life is a collection of battles.* Subsequently, it is also a collection of victories.

- ❏ Reach down deep inside yourself today and call forth your greatest strength.

- ❏ Today is not a day for weakness. *It is time to be tough.*

WISDOM WORDS

"If thou faint in the day of adversity, thy strength is small."   Proverbs 24:10

"A wise man is strong; yea, a man of knowledge increaseth strength."   Proverbs 24:5

DEPEND ON THE WISDOM OF GOD.

❑ Jesus said you have received two gifts from God: (1) Your mouth and (2) His Wisdom.

❑ Unexpected things may happen today. *Don't worry.* The Holy Spirit within you will rise to the occasion and speak through you.

❑ Relax. Someone greater than you is within you. *Depend on Him.*

WISDOM WORDS

"Settle it therefore in your hearts, not to meditate before what ye shall answer: For I will give you a mouth and wisdom, which all your adversaries shall not be able to gainsay nor resist."   Luke 21:14-15

REFUSE GRASSHOPPER TALK.

- ☐ Moses sent 12 men to spy out the land of Canaan.

- ☐ Ten of the spies came back speaking words of defeat. "We're nothing. We are like grasshoppers next to those huge giants." These ten were *grasshoppers*.

- ☐ However, the remaining two were giant-killers. Joshua and Caleb refused grasshopper talk. Instead they declared, "We are well able to overcome the giants." God gave them the land.

WISDOM WORDS

"And they brought up an evil report of the land which they had searched unto the children of Israel, saying... And there we saw the giants...and we were in our own sight as grasshoppers, and so we were in their sight."

Numbers 13:32-33

GIVE GOD TIME.

❑ Jesus invested His first 30 years in preparation for His ministry. Moses spent 80 years becoming a great leader.

❑ Time is your friend. *Don't hurry.*

❑ Remember—*Patience is the weapon that forces deception to reveal itself.*

WISDOM WORDS

"The Lord is good unto them that wait for Him, to the soul that seeketh Him. It is good that a man should both hope and quietly wait for the salvation of the Lord."
Lamentations 3:25-26

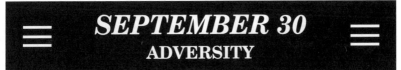
AIM YOUR SEED TOWARD DELIVERANCE TODAY.

❑ *Offerings impress God.* They always have. They always will.

❑ David understood this, and *aimed his Seed like an arrow* to get a message to God.

❑ *It worked.* The plague was *stopped.* So when you plant a special Seed-faith offering to the work of God, expect incredible favor.

WISDOM WORDS

"And David built there an altar unto the Lord, and offered burnt offerings and peace offerings. So the Lord was entreated for the land, and the plague was stayed from Israel."   2 Samuel 24:25

REACH FOR PROSPERITY.

❑ *You will never possess anything you are unwilling to pursue.*

❑ It is good to pursue good health, happiness and financial blessings. Your Heavenly Father wants you to experience all the blessings.

❑ Get ready today to launch the greatest chapter you have ever known: *PROSPERITY.*

WISDOM WORDS

"Beloved, I wish above all things that thou mayest prosper and be in health, even as thy soul prospereth."
3 John 1:2

STAY IN THE CENTER OF YOUR EXPERTISE.

❑ Even in your mother's womb you were given by God special gifts, talents and skills.

❑ *What you enjoy doing the most is a clue to what God wants you to do with your life.*

❑ Start today to build your *daily agenda* around this Assignment.

WISDOM WORDS

"Let every man abide in the same calling wherein he was called."   1 Corinthians 7:20

DO WHAT YOU LOVE.

❏ *Whatever brings you the most fulfillment is an important key to your life.*

❏ God wants you happy. That is a settled issue. Now find what makes you happy.

❏ *You will have extraordinary success with something that becomes your obsession.*

WISDOM WORDS

"Wherefore I perceive that there is nothing better, than that a man should rejoice in his own works; for that is his portion..."   Ecclesiastes 3:22

PINPOINT YOUR NEEDS.

❑ *List your personal financial needs.* These may include money for your home, your children's education, or whatever.

❑ *Your faith will begin to respond to this specific target.*

❑ Now, hold this list before the Lord. *Wrap your faith around it* and watch Jehovah-Jireh, your Provider, begin to move in your life.

WISDOM WORDS

"But my God shall supply all your need according to His riches in glory by Christ Jesus." Philippians 4:19

BECOME DEBT-FREE.

❑ Financial pressure is devastating to a marriage and family. It is considered the major cause of divorce.

❑ *Make a list* of all your debts today.

❑ Now, focus your faith and efforts toward moving this mountain. Your life is worth it.

WISDOM WORDS

"The rich ruleth over the poor, and the borrower is servant to the lender." Proverbs 22:7

ASK THE GIVER.

❑ *Everything comes from somebody.*

❑ Whatever you need...*already exists.*

❑ *Ask*. Ask with *joy*. Somebody wants to reveal His power to you.

— *WISDOM WORDS* —

"Or what man is there of you, whom if his son ask bread, will he give him a stone? Or if he ask a fish, will he give him a serpent? If ye then, being evil, know how to give good gifts unto your children, how much more shall your Father which is in heaven give good things to them that ask Him?"   Matthew 7:9-11

CONSULT THE LEARNED.

❑ *The difference between today and your future is information.*

❑ If you don't learn anything new today, tomorrow will be just like today. This means you don't have a future…just a *longer today*.

❑ So, read…listen…observe. *Your future is in your discoveries.*

WISDOM WORDS

"Where no counsel is, the people fall: but in the multitude of counsellors there is safety."

Proverbs 11:14

THINK AHEAD.

❑ I call it *"The Law of Inevitable Eventuality."*

❑ If you eat two slices of pecan pie every night, what is the *inevitable eventuality?* If you smoke two packs of cigarettes a day, what is the *inevitable eventuality?*

❑ Whatever you are doing right now...*is producing an inevitable future.* Think, think, think...*ahead.*

WISDOM WORDS

"Go to the ant, thou sluggard; consider her ways, and be wise: Which having no guide, overseer, or ruler, Provideth her meat in the summer, and gathereth her food in the harvest."   Proverbs 6:6-8

DISCOVER YOUR REAL SOURCE.

❑ *You don't have a thing God didn't give you.*

❑ Never forget it. Don't get cocky and arrogant about the little 10% tithe you give to God—He's the one that gave the 100% you have.

❑ *He is your Total Source.* He knows it. Champions know it, too.

WISDOM WORDS

"And when thy herds and thy flocks multiply, and thy silver and thy gold is multiplied, and all that thou hast is multiplied; But thou shalt remember the Lord thy God: for it is He that giveth thee power to get wealth"
Deuteronomy 8:13,18

DON'T RUSH IT.

- ❑ *Great things take time.*

- ❑ Human pregnancy takes nine months. Jesus' preparation for ministry took 30 years.

- ❑ *Willingly pace yourself on the Journey to Prosperity.* Your *present* joy depends on it.

— WISDOM WORDS —

"He that hasteth to be rich hath an evil eye, and considereth not that poverty shall come upon him."

Proverbs 28:22

KEEP GOOD RECORDS.

❑ *Accountability is vital in today's world.*

❑ Balance your checkbook *regularly.* Keep necessary *receipts* of your purchases.

❑ *Information that is not retrievable is not usable.* Keep clean records.

WISDOM WORDS

"Be thou diligent to know the state of thy flocks, and look well to thy herds. For riches are not for ever..."

Proverbs 27:23-24

TITHE WITH EXPECTATION.

- ❑ Tithe means "tenth." Abraham brought ten percent of his income back to God in thanksgiving for the blessing of God.

- ❑ This tithe is "Holy Seed."

- ❑ As you bring your tithe to God this week, wrap your faith and *expectation* around it and *look for the promised Harvest.*

WISDOM WORDS

"Bring ye all the tithes into the storehouse, that there may be meat in Mine house, and prove Me now herewith, saith the Lord of hosts, if I will not open you the windows of heaven, and pour you out a blessing, that there shall not be room enough to receive it. And I will rebuke the devourer for your sakes, and he shall not destroy the fruits of your ground..."   Malachi 3:10-11

CELEBRATE YOUR SEED.

☐ It is thrilling that Offering Time is becoming a happy and joyous occasion in many churches today.

☐ Many knowledgeable pastors are even "Celebrating The Seed"...by having their entire congregation *bring their tithes and offerings forward to the altar* each Sunday morning.

☐ *Celebrate* your Seed. *Your Father does.*

WISDOM WORDS

"For the Seed shall be prosperous; the vine shall give her fruit, and the ground shall give her increase, and the heavens shall give their dew; and I will cause the remnant of this people to possess all these things."
Zechariah 8:12

STOP SPENDING MORE THAN YOU EARN.

- ❑ *It is possible to live on less and still be happy.*

- ❑ The missing ingredient in much "prosperity teaching" is...*temperance* in all things.

- ❑ *Buying on credit is merely stripping your future to enhance your present.* Slow down and start living within your means.

WISDOM WORDS

"And every man that striveth for the mastery is temperate in all things..."   1 Corinthians 9:25

DON'T WASTE TIME.

❑ Time is precious. It is life itself. *When you waste your time, you are wasting your life.*

❑ *Managing your time wisely* is one of the most important keys to financial prosperity.

❑ Keep a *written list* of your daily tasks. Link each task to a *specific time.* This creates order—the accurate arrangement of things. *It is the Power Key to Productivity.*

WISDOM WORDS

"Redeeming the time, because the days are evil."

Ephesians 5:16

DON'T MAKE QUICK DECISIONS.

❑ *Your entire life hinges on the decisions you make.*

❑ Your decisions will create tragedies or joy. Laughter or tears. Pain or pleasure.

❑ Don't let anyone rush you into any decision before you are prepared. Be patient. *Remember, patience is the weapon that forces deception to reveal itself.*

WISDOM WORDS

"Wherefore, my beloved brethren, let every man be swift to hear, slow to speak, slow to wrath:" James 1:19

HONOR YOUR WORD.

- ❑ Truth is the most powerful force on earth. *It cannot be changed.*

- ❑ Be honest. Cherish your integrity. Keep your word.

- ❑ *Never make a promise impossible to keep.*

WISDOM WORDS

"A good name is rather to be chosen than great riches, and loving favour rather than silver and gold."

Proverbs 22:1

BRAINSTORM FOR CREATIVE IDEAS.

❑ *God has countless and varied ways to get finances into your hands.*

❑ Sit down today with two creative friends. Together, pray for God to give you the greatest financial ideas you have ever birthed.

❑ Write them down. *God will teach you to profit.*

WISDOM WORDS

"Thus saith the Lord, thy Redeemer, the Holy One of Israel; I am the Lord thy God which teacheth thee to profit, which leadeth thee by the way that thou shouldest go." Isaiah 48:17

BE FAITHFUL IN THE LITTLE THINGS.

- ❑ *Little hinges swing big doors.* Acorns produce oak trees.

- ❑ *Little things really do matter.* Develop a passion for *details*.

- ❑ Just do the basics: Keep a budget, balance your checkpoint, pay your bills on time, plant your Seeds in the work of God, *expect to see miracles every day of your life.*

WISDOM WORDS

"Well done, good and faithful servant; thou hast been faithful over a few things, I will make thee ruler over many things"   Matthew 25:23

STAY HEALTHY.

❑ *Energy is a major ingredient for success.*

❑ Respect your body. Listen to it. *When fatigue walks in, faith walks out.*

❑ A well-known doctor, famous for treating depression patients, said he had never had a depressed patient who was really physically fit. *What you spend your time on is what you truly respect.*

WISDOM WORDS

"And ye shall serve the Lord your God, and He shall bless thy bread, and thy water; and I will take sickness away from the midst of thee."   Exodus 23:25

NETWORK WITH OTHERS.

❑ Remember, *one cannot multiply.*

❑ Develop people-skills. Listen. Learn. Absorb from others. Ask questions. Document answers.

❑ *Success is a collection of relationships.* Whatever you are willing to settle for, determines the *quality of your future.*

WISDOM WORDS

"Two are better than one; because they have a good reward for their labour. For if they fall, the one will lift up his fellow: but woe to him that is alone when he falleth; for he hath not another to help him up."

Ecclesiastes 4:9-10

DRAW UP A DETAILED PLAN.

❑ *Your vision is your future.*

❑ The Bible is God's written List of Goals. He wrote down what He wanted to happen.

❑ It may be difficult for you to transfer your thoughts on paper, but do it. *Something wonderful starts happening when you actually see a blueprint of your future.*

WISDOM WORDS

"Write the vision, and make it plain upon tables, that he may run that readeth it."   Habakkuk 2:2

"Where there is no vision, the people perish"
                                             Proverbs 29:18

DETERMINE TO BE DILIGENT.

❑ *Diligence is speedy attention to an assigned task.*

❑ Respond *immediately* to your supervisor's instructions. Don't wait. Act.

❑ According to the Bible, *this is a key element to every promotion*. So, move...move...*move quickly* to your assigned tasks.

WISDOM WORDS

"He becometh poor that dealeth with a slack hand: but the hand of the diligent maketh rich."   Proverbs 10:4

DON'T WASTE MONEY.

❏ You often hear that billionaires are stingy. Some are even known to bring their own lunch to work. They learned early to make every dollar count.

❏ What you do with $10.00 is what you will eventually do with $100.00.

❏ Respect what God has given to you. *What you don't respect, you will eventually lose.*

WISDOM WORDS

"Not slothful in business; fervent in spirit; serving the Lord;"   Romans 12:11

GO THE EXTRA MILE.

❑ Jesus taught *"The Law of the Second Mile."*

❑ It simply means to do more than what is really expected of you. It means to *think* and *look* for *extra* ways to *benefit* others.

❑ Always remember—*Your rewards are determined by the kinds of problems you are willing to solve.*

WISDOM WORDS

"And whosoever shall compel thee to go a mile, go with him twain."   Matthew 5:41

PURSUE WISDOM.

❑ *Wisdom is simply doing what God would do in a given situation.*

❑ Wisdom is the Master Key to financial prosperity.

❑ Jesus is made unto us the Wisdom of God. Whatever you face today, *just do what you know Jesus would do.*

— WISDOM WORDS —

"Get wisdom, get understanding: forget it not; neither decline from the words of my mouth."   Proverbs 4:5

"Length of days is in her right hand; and in her left hand riches and honour."   Proverbs 3:16

FEAR GOD.

❑ The fear of God does not mean to be afraid of God. It means to *respect, honor and complete any instruction He gives you.*

❑ Your obedience *triggers events* that bring financial blessings. Disobedience triggers events that bring financial ruin.

❑ *The fear of the Lord is the beginning of Wisdom.*

WISDOM WORDS

"By humility and the fear of the Lord are riches, and honour, and life." Proverbs 22:4

DON'T ATTEMPT TOO MANY THINGS.

❑ A famous billionaire once said, "I've seen as many people fail from attempting too many things as I have from attempting too few."

❑ Don't overload yourself. It will *break your focus.*

❑ The real *reason men fail is broken focus.* Find something *worthy* of consuming you, and *pour your life into it.*

WISDOM WORDS

"A double minded man is unstable in all his ways."

James 1:8

LOOK FOR A PROBLEM TO SOLVE.

❑ *Everything God has made is a solution to a problem.*

❑ *Your worth and significance are determined by the kinds of problems you are solving for someone.* If you want to earn $100.00 an hour, you must find a $100.00 an hour problem to solve.

❑ Your significance is not your similarity to others. It is your *difference.* Find your *point of difference…*and *solve a problem with it.* Prosperity is inevitable.

— *WISDOM WORDS* —

"Withhold not good from them to whom it is due, when it is in the power of thine hand to do it."

Proverbs 3:27

REMEMBER THE POOR.

☐ Thousands are homeless, destitute and impoverished.

☐ *Your reaction to them determines God's reaction to you.*

☐ Get involved. Plant your best Seed in a church or worthy organization committed to the poor. Your own prosperity will be affected by it.

— WISDOM WORDS —

"He that hath pity upon the poor lendeth unto the Lord; and that which he hath given will He pay him again."
Proverbs 19:17

"Blessed is he that considereth the poor: the Lord will deliver him in time of trouble. The Lord will preserve him, and keep him alive; and he shall be blessed upon the earth: and Thou wilt not deliver him unto the will of his enemies." Psalm 41:1,2

ENLARGE YOUR CORNER.

❑ God instructed the wealthy to leave barley and wheat in the corners of their fields for the poor and needy.

❑ Your *field* is anything God has given to you. Your *corner* is anything you are giving back to God.

❑ Your field is your *income*. Your corner is your *outgo*. *The larger you make your corner, the larger God will make your field.* It is just a matter of *time*.

WISDOM WORDS

"And when ye reap the harvest of your land, thou shalt not wholly reap the corners of thy field, neither shalt thou gather the gleanings of thy harvest. And thou shalt not glean thy vineyard, neither shalt thou gather every grape of thy vineyard; thou shalt leave them for the poor and stranger: I am the Lord your God."

Leviticus 19:9-10

MAKE PRAYER TIME AN APPOINTMENT TIME.

❑ Two unforgettable disciples, Peter and John, kept their prayer appointment with God.

❑ Daniel prayed three times daily. The psalmist prayed seven times daily. *Great men simply have great habits.*

❑ You make appointments with lawyers, doctors and friends. *Start making daily appointments with God.*

── WISDOM WORDS ──

"Now Peter and John went up together into the temple at the hour of prayer, being the ninth hour."　Acts 3:1

ARM YOURSELF WITH SCRIPTURE.

- ❑ *God always remembers what He says.*

- ❑ He responds favorably to you when *you* remember what He says.

- ❑ When you approach God, He wants you to remind Him of His promises to you.

WISDOM WORDS

"If ye abide in Me, and My words abide in you, ye shall ask what ye will, and it shall be done unto you."

John 15:7

DEVELOP DISCIPLINE.

❑ *The secret of your future is hidden in your daily routine.*

❑ Great achievers have success routines they follow diligently. They simply discipline themselves for a period of time *until a daily habit is born.*

❑ Develop a rhythm for your prayer life. It is the heartbeat of your spiritual life.

WISDOM WORDS

"As for me, I will call upon God; and the Lord shall save me. Evening, and morning, and at noon, will I pray, and cry aloud: and He shall hear my voice."

Psalm 55:16-17

BELONG TO A PRAYER GROUP.

❑ Your private prayer life is powerful.

❑ However the Bible says that when two pray, something even more powerful takes place.

❑ Find a prayer group or birth a new group in your neighborhood or church. It could be the greatest contribution of your entire life.

WISDOM WORDS

"For where two or three are gathered together in My name, there am I in the midst of them."

Matthew 18:20

CHOOSE A PRAYER PARTNER.

❑ You cannot trust everyone with your private thoughts or problems.

❑ But, you need *someone.* One cannot multiply. Two is the secret to multiplication.

❑ Jesus introduced the Formula for Prayer Power. It's called the prayer of agreement. *Don't ignore it.*

— *WISDOM WORDS* —

"Again I say unto you, That if two of you shall agree on earth as touching any thing that they shall ask, it shall be done for them of My Father which is in heaven."

Matthew 18:19

DECIDE YOUR TRUE DESIRES.

- ❑ Few people really know what they want in life.

- ❑ *Name your needs.* Determine your burning desires.

- ❑ Now, speak them aloud to God. Boldly. *Expectantly.* Decisiveness is in your favor today.

WISDOM WORDS

"But without faith it is impossible to please Him; for he that cometh to God must believe that He is, and that He is a rewarder of them that diligently seek Him."

Hebrews 11:6

ELIMINATE DISTRACTIONS.

❑ *Atmosphere matters.* Protecting your focus is critical in releasing your faith.

❑ Separate yourself unto the Lord. Disconnect from outside influences.

❑ *Unclutter your hour of prayer.* Miracles are at stake.

WISDOM WORDS

"But thou, when thou prayest, enter into thy closet, and when thou hast shut thy door, pray to thy Father which is in secret; and thy Father which seeth in secret shall reward thee openly."   Matthew 6:6

USE SATAN AS A MEMO PAD.

❑ Every time you enter your prayer time, satan will remind you of something you forgot to do. It may be a telephone call to make, a letter to write, but it is designed to *break your focus.*

❑ *Keep a memo pad and pen handy as you pray.* When satan reminds you of something, simply write it down for later. Then say, "Thank you satan for being my memo pad."

❑ Now relax and enjoy your time with God.

WISDOM WORDS

"Lest Satan should get an advantage of us: for we are not ignorant of his devices." 2 Corinthians 2:11

DON'T EDIT.

- ❏ *God already knows everything about you.*

- ❏ When you pray, be direct. Be honest. He rewards integrity.

- ❏ *Talk it out.* You can trust the One Who made you. He's got all the time in the world. *Don't edit* your conversation with Him.

WISDOM WORDS

"And ye shall seek Me, and find Me, when ye shall search for Me with all your heart."   Jeremiah 29:13

ENJOY HIS PRESENCE.

❏ *When you get into the presence of God, something happens that does not happen anywhere else.*

❏ Bring to Him your fears, worries, doubts and tears. You greatly matter to Him today. You really do.

❏ So, enjoy Him. He currently enjoys you.

WISDOM WORDS

"Thou wilt shew me the path of life: in Thy presence is fulness of joy; at Thy right hand there are pleasures for evermore." Psalm 16:11

EXPECT AN ANSWER.

❑ *Faith is confidence in God.*

❑ *Faith comes when God talks.* It may be through a ministry, the Holy Spirit or His word.

❑ *Expectation is the invisible current that sweeps miracles into your life.*

WISDOM WORDS

"And it shall come to pass, that before they call, I will answer; and while they are yet speaking, I will hear."

Isaiah 65:24

EXPRESS YOURSELF FREELY.

❑ *Never be ashamed of your emotions.*

❑ God is emotional. You are made in His image.

❑ When you get into His presence, you can say anything you want...any way you want to say it. He is simply thrilled you have come for a visit.

— WISDOM WORDS —

"And at the evening sacrifice I arose up from my heaviness; and having rent my garment and my mantle, I fell upon my knees, and spread out my hands unto the Lord my God,"   Ezra 9:5

PICTURE YOUR MIRACLE.

❑ *God begins everything with a picture.*

❑ God pointed out the stars to Abraham to stir his faith for children. The woman diseased for 12 years saw a picture in her heart and it moved her to touch the robe of Jesus.

❑ Guard well the Miracle Picture God has placed within you. It is the *key* to your miracle.

WISDOM WORDS

"For she said within herself, If I may but touch His garment, I shall be whole."   Matthew 9:21

PRAY YOUR EXPECTATIONS.

- ❏ *Words matter.* They create death or life.

- ❏ Your mind and your faith respond to anything you say.

- ❏ *Never verbalize anything you don't really want to happen.* Pray your expectations, not your experiences.

WISDOM WORDS

"For verily I say unto you, That whosoever shall say unto this mountain, Be thou removed, and be thou cast into the sea; and shall not doubt in his heart, but shall believe that those things which he saith shall come to pass; he shall have whatsoever he saith."

Mark 11:23

DON'T SABOTAGE A YESTERDAY PRAYER.

❏ Let's suppose you have just asked God for the salvation of your mate or loved one.

❏ He heard you. It mattered. He has promised a response.

❏ *Events are now in motion.* Don't come back today and speak words of doubt and unbelief to God or others. You may paralyze everything God is doing.

WISDOM WORDS

"But let him ask in faith, nothing wavering. For he that wavereth is like a wave of the sea driven with the wind and tossed."   James 1:6

ESTABLISH A PLACE FOR PRAYER.

❑ *Places matter to God.* He made them too, you know.

❑ Think of these places: The Upper Room, Jericho, Bethel, Zarapheth, Gethsemane.

❑ Jesus had special *places* for prayer. Mountains. Gethsemane. Go ahead…sanctify your own personal Prayer Place. It will become a precious and treasured Place.

WISDOM WORDS

"And when He had sent the multitudes away, He went up into a mountain apart to pray: and when the evening was come, He was there alone."   Matthew 14:23

PRAY IN THE NAME OF JESUS.

❑ Our creator is interested in order.

❑ Remember, order is the accurate arrangement of things. *Approaching God requires spiritual protocol.*

❑ When you talk to the Father, come to Him…"In the name of Jesus."

WISDOM WORDS

"If ye shall ask any thing in My name, I will do it."
John 14:14

KEEP A PRAYER LIST.

❑ Great intercessors often keep a map or globe of the world in their prayer room. They lay their hands on certain countries or cities as a *point-of-contact*.

❑ Others keep a *list of names* in the back of their Bible. It is a visual reminder to them.

❑ Since you are serious about effective praying, start your own Personal Prayer list today.

WISDOM WORDS

"I thank God, Whom I serve from my forefathers with pure conscience, that without ceasing I have remembrance of thee in my prayers night and day;"

2 Timothy 1:3

LOOSE YOUR PRAYER LANGUAGE.

❑ French. German. Spanish. English. It is only natural that the Creator who thought of all the languages of the world...*has one of His own.*

❑ It is often called "a Heavenly language." It is a personal and powerful communication between a believer and his Father.

❑ Don't allow prejudice to rob you of this experience. *Explore its possibilities.*

WISDOM WORDS

"For he that speaketh in an unknown tongue speaketh not unto men, but unto God: for no man understandeth him; howbeit in the spirit he speaketh mysteries."

1 Corinthians 14:2

LEARN SIX LEVELS OF THE LORD'S PRAYER.

❑ Jesus taught His disciples *how* to pray.

❑ There are six levels: 1) Praise 2) Priorities 3)Provisions 4) Pardon 5) Protection and 6) Praise, again.

❑ This little System for Prayer is quite powerful. Carefully and expectantly pray this prayer aloud today. *He taught it to us.*

WISDOM WORDS

"After this manner therefore pray ye: Our Father which art in heaven, Hallowed be Thy name. Thy kingdom come. Thy will be done in earth, as it is in heaven. Give us this day our daily bread. And forgive us our debts, as we forgive our debtors. And lead us not into temptation, but deliver us from evil: For Thine is the kingdom, and the power, and the glory, for ever. Amen."
Matthew 6:9-13

FOCUS ON PRAISE.

❑ When Jesus taught His disciples how to pray, His first focus was on *entering the presence of God with praise.*

❑ He drew attention to the *Name of God.*

❑ So, today, begin praising God aloud for being Jehovah-Jireh (Provider), Jehovah-Shilom (Peace), Jehovah-Rophe (Healer), Jehovah-Nissi (Banner), Jehovah-Rohi (Shepherd), Jehovah-Tsidkenu (Righteousness).

WISDOM WORDS

"After this manner therefore pray ye: Our Father which art in heaven, Hallowed be Thy name."   Matthew 6:9

FOCUS ON PRIORITIES.

☐ "Let's pray this Prayer together: "Father, I set myself in agreement that the will of God shall be done today...in my government...in my church...on my job...and within my home and family.

☐ "You see my written list of things to do. You know *the people* I am meeting today. Remove those who do not belong on my schedule. I speak to the north, the south, east and west, and call forth from the shadows of my life those you have intended to be linked with me.

☐ "Father, *Your priorities* are mine. *Your will* shall be done. I am led by your peace, filled with your joy and controlled by the Holy Spirit. In Jesus' Name, Amen."

WISDOM WORDS

"Thy kingdom come. Thy will be done in earth, as it is in heaven."   Matthew 6:10

FOCUS ON PROVISIONS.

❑ Let's pray this Prayer together: "Heavenly Father, You are Jehovah-Jirah, my Provider. *Everything I have came from You.* Everything *in my future* will come from You. I don't have a thing You did not give to me.

❑ "Thank You for bringing the provisions I need for today. I trust You. My Seed is in Your Hand. That is the proof I trust You.

❑ "You are a Miracle God Who provides supernaturally all the finances I need for today. It is done in Jesus' Name, Amen."

WISDOM WORDS

"Give us this day our daily bread."   Matthew 6:11

FOCUS ON PARDON.

❑ Let's pray this Prayer together: "I thank you, Lord, for pardon, mercy and forgiveness. Thank You for forgiving me of my sins, my transgressions, my mistakes. Your peace and joy are filling me up as evidence that my record is spotless because of the righteousness of Jesus.

❑ "Today, I forgive those who have sinned against me, hurt me and cause me harm in any way. I forgive them gladly because You showed mercy to me, and the servant is not above his Lord.

❑ "I will walk in love, and forgive in advance anyone who may wrong me today. In Jesus' Name, Amen."

WISDOM WORDS

"And forgive us our debts, as we forgive our debtors."
Matthew 6:12

FOCUS ON PROTECTION.

❑ Let's pray this Prayer together: "Father, You will guide me away from temptation today and any trap planned by satan to destroy my life.

❑ "You will deliver me from any strategy to harm me in any way. Thank You for Divine and angelic protection.

❑ "I have planted Seeds of faith that guarantee You will rebuke any devourer that rises up against my life. In Jesus' Name, Amen."

WISDOM WORDS

"And lead us not into temptation, but deliver us from evil: For Thine is the kingdom, and the power, and the glory, forever. Amen."   Matthew 6:13

FOCUS ON PRAISE AGAIN.

❑ Let's pray this Prayer together: "Father, I praise You again for influencing my *PRIORITIES* today...for *PROVISIONS*...for *PARDON* of every sin...for *PROTECTION* from every evil work.

❑ "Now Your praise shall continually be in my mouth... You are my Healer, Deliverer, Savior and Miracle-Worker.

❑ "I choose to trust You completely. You will not disappoint me. In Jesus' Name, Amen."

WISDOM WORDS

"And lead us not into temptation, but deliver us from evil: For Thine is the kingdom, and the power, and the glory, forever. Amen."   Matthew 6:13

STUDY THE CHAMPIONS OF PRAYER.

❑ *Heroes are worth observing.*

❑ The Bible is a Book of Champions. Read it carefully and you will see a parade of extraordinary people who changed the course of history *through their prayer life.*

❑ David, Daniel, Esther, Moses and Elijah are only part of the thousands of Champions...*study their lives.*

WISDOM WORDS

"Elias was a man subject to like passions as we are, and he prayed earnestly that it might not rain: and it rained not on the earth by the space of three years and six months."   James 5:17

CONCLUDE TELEPHONE CONVERSATIONS WITH PRAYER.

❏ *Conversations are opportunities.*

❏ When you finish your telephone conversations today, simply say, "Let's have a brief word of prayer before I go."

❏ "Father, you've listened to what concerns us. We invite Your influence and trust You for a miracle. Amen." *You have now provided God an Entry Point for a miracle.*

WISDOM WORDS

"Rejoice evermore...Pray without ceasing."

1 Thessalonians 5:16,17

LET GOD DO HIS WORK.

❏ *Someone arrived here before you.* Your Creator.

❏ The composer has written his own song. The artist has painted his own masterpiece. *God has planned His own world.* Never forget it.

❏ *Get out of His way.* He is not a beginner. He will finish what He has started.

WISDOM WORDS

"The Lord will perfect that which concerneth me: Thy mercy, O Lord, endureth for ever: forsake not the works of Thine own hands." Psalm 138:8

REPENT QUICKLY.

❑ Your mistakes and sins have not shocked God. He anticipated your need for mercy.

❑ *The Master Key to Recovery is Repentance.*

❑ Don't justify yourself. Quit blaming others for the decisions you have made. Repent. *Immediately*.

WISDOM WORDS

"He that covereth his sins shall not prosper: but whoso confesseth and forsaketh them shall have mercy."

Proverbs 28:13

RESPECT YOUR TONGUE.

- ❑ When God wanted to create the world...He *spoke*.

- ❑ Words are creative forces that *bring* into existence that which never existed before.

- ❑ Your tongue is one of the greatest gifts placed at your command by God. Use it *wisely* and you will discover the golden key to life.

— WISDOM WORDS —

"Behold also the ships, which though they be so great, and are driven of fierce winds, yet are they turned about with a very small helm, whithersoever the governor listeth. Even so the tongue is a little member, and boasteth great things. Behold, how great a matter a little fire kindleth!"   James 3:4-5

SAY WHAT GOD WANTS TO HEAR.

- ❑ Your words *affect* God. Your prayers *ignite* God.

- ❑ Jesus taught His disciples *how* to pray...for provision, protection and pardon (Matthew 6:9-13).

- ❑ *Faith-talk* is what God responds to favorably. Confess your sins...your desire for forgiveness...*and* the things you need God to do in your life.

WISDOM WORDS

"If My people, which are called by My name, shall humble themselves, and pray, and seek My face, and turn from their wicked ways; then will I hear from heaven, and will forgive their sin, and will heal their land."   2 Chronicles 7:14

TALK TO YOURSELF.

- ❑ *External* communication is what you say to *others*. *Internal* communication is what you say to *yourself*.

- ❑ Others may not talk the Good Report to you...so talk it to yourself!

- ❑ What you say — about your enemy, your future, your expectations—*affects what you believe.*

── WISDOM WORDS ──

"This book of the law shall not depart out of thy mouth; but thou shalt meditate therein day and night, that thou mayest observe to do according to all that is written therein: for then thou shalt make thy way prosperous, and then thou shalt have good success." Joshua 1:8

TALK EXPECTATIONS NOT EXPERIENCES.

❑ Do not drag yesterday into your future.

❑ Perhaps you have just been *fired* from your job. Do not major on your feeling of rejection. Instead, point out the possibility of promotion and changes of freedom that suddenly may emerge.

❑ Nurture the Photographs of Possibilities within your heart. Elijah gave the widow of Zarephath a picture of her potential. It stirred her expectations of a miracle Harvest in her life (1 Kings 17).

WISDOM WORDS

"And let us not be weary in well doing: for in due season we shall reap, if we faint not." Galatians 6:9

ABSORB THE PROMISES OF GOD.

❑ Study the Covenant God established with those who talk in obedience to Him.

❑ You can only operate in faith according to your knowledge of His will or desire for your life. For example, if you do not know that God has already provided for your healing, how can you believe Him for a miracle in your health?

❑ You must have a clear photograph of the will of God so your faith can implement it.

WISDOM WORDS

"He that cometh to God must believe that He is, and that He is a rewarder of them that diligently seek Him."
Hebrews 11:6

PICTURE YOUR DESIRED FUTURE.

❑ Abraham had a picture of many generations of children he wanted (Genesis 17).

❑ Joseph had a dream of himself as a leader and he *remembered* it (Genesis 37).

❑ Know God's dream for your life. Get The Picture. Big. *BIGGER*. Fill up your mind, heart and life with it. Now make that vision consume your life…every conversation…ever thought…everything around you.

WISDOM WORDS

"Where there is no vision, the people perish: but he that keepeth the law, happy is he."　　Proverbs 29:18

FIND FAITH FOOD.

❑ What you *read* affects what you believe.

❑ When you feed the scriptures into your spirit man, faith comes alive and becomes a living force.

❑ Read the Bible. Read books that stir your faith in God. Nurture the Seed of Faith inside you. Acorns become oak trees.

WISDOM WORDS

"So then faith cometh by hearing, and hearing by the word of God."   Romans 10:17

LISTEN TO MENTORS OF FAITH.

❑ Joshua learned under Moses.
Timothy learned under Paul.
Elisha learned under Elijah.

❑ Observe successful lives carefully. Secrets will surface. Reasons for their success will emerge.

❑ Read biographies of extraordinary people who tapped into the Fountain of Faith. Their lives will excite you to new heights of faith.

WISDOM WORDS

"Wherefore seeing we also are compassed about with so great a cloud of witnesses, let us lay aside every weight, and the sin which doth so easily beset us, and let us run with patience the race that is set before us,"

Hebrews 12:1

DECEMBER 9
FAITH-TALK

REFLECT ON THE VICTORIES OF BIBLE CHAMPIONS.

❏ David, with a simple slingshot, killed Goliath and eventually became king (1 Samuel 17).

❏ Joseph overcame the hatred of his brothers, false accusation and became second in power to Pharaoh (Genesis 37-41).

❏ Ponder and meditate on the lives of such champions …it will unleash energy, enthusiasm and faith.

WISDOM WORDS

"…the people that do know their God shall be strong, and do exploits."　　　　　　　　Daniel 11:32

LOOSEN UP AND LAUGH.

❑ You are being observed today. Satan is watching to see if his tactics are working.

❑ *Laugh* aloud and rejoice that your circumstances are attracting the attention of God, too.

❑ Miracles are always birthed when things seem their worst. Satan is sensitive and very capable of being discouraged. So…make the effort to rejoice.

WISDOM WORDS

"A merry heart doeth good like a medicine: but a broken spirit drieth the bones."   Proverbs 17:22

REPLAY SUCCESS IN YOUR MIND.

❑ Think about *your* past battles and struggles.

❑ David *remembered* and *replayed* his victories over the bear and lion...*before* he ran toward Goliath (1 Samuel 17:37).

❑ Yesterday is your history successes. *Remember* them. *Talk* about them. Satan is the only one you will irritate!

WISDOM WORDS

"...Joshua said...take you up every man...a stone upon his shoulder...That this may be a sign...that when your children ask...What mean ye by these stones? Then ye shall answer them, That the waters of Jordan were cut off before the ark of the covenant...and these stones shall be for a memorial unto the children of Israel for ever."

Joshua 4:5-7

KEEP A JOURNAL OF MIRACLES.

❑ God instructed Israel to pile stones to *remind their children* of the greatness of God (Joshua 4:4-10).

❑ *Look* for miracles everyday...unexpected, unplanned introductions to people; information that suddenly emerges; an invitation that opens great doors of opportunities.

❑ Document these experiences *daily*. Your written journal is your private *reservoir of memories* that feed your faith.

WISDOM WORDS

"...the Lord said unto Moses, Write this for a memorial in a book, and rehearse it in the ears of Joshua"
Exodus 17:14

MAKE IT A POINT TO BE THANKFUL.

- ❏ Thankfulness produces *joy*.

- ❏ It does not take a genius to locate, discern and detect flaws. However, it takes great awareness to see the good things of life.

- ❏ *Savor* God's everyday blessings. Your eyesight, your hearing, your ability to speak…and the thousands of things to be happy about.

WISDOM WORDS

"…for the joy of the Lord is your strength."

Nehemiah 8:10

"…when they knew God, they glorified Him not as God, neither were thankful; but became vain in their imaginations, and their foolish heart was darkened."

Romans 1:21

SAVOR EACH MOMENT.

- ❑ Savor means to *taste, feel* and *extract* all the pleasure and benefit…of each moment.

- ❑ Someone has well said, "You are going to be on the journey longer than you will be at the destination …so, enjoy the journey."

- ❑ *Always be where you are.* Do not permit your mind to race miles ahead of where your body is. Taste *now*… it is the future you have been talking about your entire life.

WISDOM WORDS

"…now is the accepted time; behold, now is the day of salvation." 2 Corinthians 6:2

TURN LITTLE BLESSINGS INTO CELEBRATIONS.

❑ Gorgeous sunsets. Laughter of children. Hot bubble baths. Vacant parking space at the mall. *Celebrate each little blessing.*

❑ Life is a *journey.* Focus on all the little things that make it pleasurable. Do not take today for granted.

❑ You have *already* received…and received…and received so much from God. *Talk it up!*

WISDOM WORDS

"Giving thanks always for all things unto God and the Father in the name of our Lord Jesus Christ;"

Ephesians 5:20

MAKE TODAY A MAJOR EVENT IN YOUR LIFE.

- ❏ Do not be passive today. You are *alive! Act* like it!! *Talk* like it!! *Celebrate* yourself!!

- ❏ Speak a little *louder* today. Speak a little *faster*.

- ❏ Smile *bigger*…laugh *aloud*…and exude the joy of Jesus as you spread it generously over every single hour today.

WISDOM WORDS

"This is the day which the Lord hath made; we will rejoice and be glad in it."   Psalm 118:24

POUR THE WORD OVER YOUR MIND DAILY.

❑ Your mind gathers the dirt, grime and dust of human opinion every day.

❑ Renew your mind to the *truth*—God's Word. Schedule an appointment with the Bible *daily*. The *renewing* of your mind is the key to *changes* within you.

❑ The Words of God are like waterfalls...*washing* and purifying your mind.

WISDOM WORDS

"That he might sanctify and cleanse it with the washing of water by the word,"   Ephesians 5:26

PUT FAITH SIGNS IN YOUR HOUSE.

❑ What you see determines what you *feel*.

❑ So, put a little sign on your refrigerator, bathroom mirror and bulletin boards to *stir your faith*.

❑ God instructed the children of Israel to put up His Word as signs before their eyes on the door posts of their homes (Deuteronomy 11:18-25).

WISDOM WORDS

"Mine eye affecteth mine heart"   Lamentations 3:51

"Therefore shall ye lay up these My words in your heart...and bind them for a sign upon your hand, that they may be as frontlets between your eyes. And thou shalt write them upon the door posts of thine house"
Deuteronomy 11:18,20

LOOK ON THE BRIGHT SIDE OF A PROBLEM.

❑ Learn to make lemonade out of every *lemon experience.*

❑ When my plane is delayed, I think of it as an extra hour to *read or catch up on correspondence.*

❑ Think...about all the potential advantages a problem might produce.

WISDOM WORDS

"Finally, brethren, whatsoever things are true, whatsoever things are honest, whatsoever things are just, whatsoever things are pure, whatsoever things are lovely, whatsoever things are of good report; if there be any virtue, and if there be any praise, think on these things."   Philippians 4:8

FOCUS ON THE REWARDS OF FINISHING A TASK.

❑ Every task has an unpleasant side...but you must cultivate focus on the *end results* you are producing.

❑ Complaining people focus on the *wrong* things... their effort, toil or responsibility.

❑ Champions talk faith because their *focus* is on the *finished results*.

WISDOM WORDS

"...he that endureth to the end shall be saved."

Matthew 10:22

ASK A DIFFERENT QUESTION.

❑ Stop asking yourself questions that do not have answers such as, *"WHY*...did this happen to me?" Or, *"WHY* do they treat me this way?"

❑ Ask yourself creative questions such as, *"WHAT* can I do immediately to create changes?" Or, *"HOW* can I improve the situation?"

❑ Your mind will struggle to produce answers to every question you ask it. So do not exhaust it. Ask the *right* questions.

WISDOM WORDS

"Ask, and it shall be given you; seek, and ye shall find; knock, and it shall be opened unto you:"

Matthew 7:7

REFUSE THE ROLE OF A VICTIM.

❑ The Victim Vocabulary includes, "I do not have an education," "I was abused in my childhood," and "My father deserted my mother…"

❑ Do not adopt this attitude. Fight it. *Yesterday is over.* Act like it.

❑ You have the anointing of God wrapped around you. You are not a captive, but a *Deliverer.* You are not a victim, but a *Victor.*

WISDOM WORDS

"Ye are of God, little children, and have overcome them: because greater is He that is in you, than he that is in the world."   1 John 4:4

ASSESS YOUR ATMOSPHERE.

❑ Indians used to wet their fingers and hold them in the wind to discern the direction of air currents.

❑ So you must learn to observe and *diagnose* the currents, climate and emotional atmosphere others are creating around you.

❑ Their words are poison or power. Their words are destructive or creative. Their words are doubt or faith building. Assess them *accurately*.

WISDOM WORDS

"And when Jesus came…He said unto them, Give place: for the maid is not dead, but sleepeth. And they laughed Him to scorn. But when the people were put forth, He went in, and took her by the hand, and the maid arose."
Matthew 9:23-25

PINPOINT YOUR SUPPORT SYSTEM.

❑ Nobody succeeds alone. *NOBODY*.

❑ Friends differ. Some *correct* you. Others *direct* you. Some make you *think*. Others make you *feel*.

❑ Pinpoint those who truly stimulate you…educate you…placate you. Meticulously build your *foundation* for friendship…a support system that is the result of *thought* instead of chance.

WISDOM WORDS

"Two are better than one…For if they fall, the one will lift up his fellow: but woe to him that is alone when he falleth; for he hath not another to help him up."

Ecclesiastes 4:9-10

SCREEN DOUBTERS.

❑ Screen doors prevent obnoxious insects from entering your home.

❑ You must assertively screen out people who are *carriers* of the virus of doubt and unbelief.

❑ Boldly protect your ears and life from absorbing talk that does not edify and build.

WISDOM WORDS

"But He turned, and said unto Peter, Get thee behind me, satan: thou art an offence unto Me: for thou savourest not the things that be of God, but those that be of men."   Matthew 16:23

"A little leaven leaveneth the whole lump."
                                        Galatians 5:9

RECOGNIZE DOUBT PRODUCES TRAGEDIES.

❑ God has *feelings*. Some words grieve His heart. Some words excite His heart. Unbelief brings God great pain. Faith brings Him great pleasure.

❑ Twelve spies analyzed Canaan for 40 days. Moses and the people accepted the Report of Doubt from the 10 spies instead of the Report of Faith from Joshua and Caleb (Numbers 13).

❑ *Each day of doubt brought 365 days of heartache. Doubt is as contagious as faith.*

WISDOM WORDS

"After the number of the days in which ye searched the land, even forty days, each day for a year, shall ye bear your iniquities, even forty years, and ye shall know my breach of promise."   Numbers 14:34

MARK CONTENTIOUS PEOPLE.

❑ *Note* those who always create conflict, complain and are hostile toward everything.

❑ Do not give them an opportunity to air their grievances and inject poison into the conversation.

❑ *Take charge.*

WISDOM WORDS

"…mark them which cause divisions and offences contrary to the doctrine which ye have learned; and avoid them."   Romans 16:17

"Cast out the scorner, and contention shall go out; yea, strife and reproach shall cease."   Proverbs 22:10

DO NOT FEED AN ARGUMENTATIVE ATTITUDE.

❑ You will be challenged today. Someone will be wanting to start an argument, a quarrel.

❑ Do not fall for it. *Refuse* to feed a contentious spirit. It erodes your keenness and *breaks your focus*.

❑ *Re-direct the conversation* to the power of God, and the potential miracle about to be birthed!

WISDOM WORDS

"A soft answer turneth away wrath: but grievous words stir up anger."   Proverbs 15:1

INDENTIFY COMPLAINERS.

❑ You will hear a lot of garbage and unbelief dumped into your ears today. *Name it for what it is.*

❑ Discern complainers. Recognize the *spirit* of murmuring that has entered someone, poisoning every conversation.

❑ *Do not participate.* Take the conversation upward by stating, "What an opportunity for God to perform a miracle!"

WISDOM WORDS

"…when the people complained, it displeased the Lord: and the Lord heard it; and His anger was kindled; and the fire of the Lord burnt among them, and consumed them that were in the uttermost parts of the camp."

Numbers 11:1

LEARN TO LINGER IN THE PRESENCE OF GOD.

❑ Those who surround you influence what you become.

❑ Something happens in the presence of God that does not happen anywhere else. *Commands* take a moment. *Plans* take time. Linger long enough to *hear His plans.*

❑ Your views will change *in His presence.* Your perceptions are corrected *in His presence.* Your faith explodes *in His presence.*

WISDOM WORDS

"Thou wilt shew me the path of life: in Thy presence is fulness of joy; at Thy right hand there are pleasures for evermore." Psalm 16:11

MAKE YOURSELF UNFORGETTABLE TO GOD.

- ❏ Conversations *reveal* what you love, hate, crave or despise is exposed by your words.

- ❏ Faith is confidence in God.

- ❏ When you speak confidently of God's integrity, and victoriously exude your anticipation of miracles... God is pleasured. God will remember you for the pleasure you created.

WISDOM WORDS
"But without faith it is impossible to please Him"
Hebrews 11:6

58 MASTER SECRETS FOR TOTAL SUCCESS

1. JESUS HAD SOMETHING OTHERS NEEDED.

2. JESUS BELIEVED IN HIS PRODUCT.

3. JESUS NEVER MISREPRESENTED HIS PRODUCT.

4. JESUS WENT WHERE THE PEOPLE WERE.

5. JESUS TOOK TIME TO REST.

6. JESUS TOOK TIME TO PLAN.

7. JESUS KNEW THAT HE DID NOT HAVE TO CLOSE EVERY SALE TO BE A SUCCESS.

8. JESUS WAS A PROBLEM-SOLVER.

9. JESUS WAS CONCERNED ABOUT PEOPLE'S FINANCES.

10. JESUS WAS WILLING TO GO WHERE HE HAD NEVER BEEN BEFORE.

11. JESUS NEVER ALLOWED WHAT OTHERS SAID ABOUT HIM TO CHANGE HIS OPINION OF HIMSELF.

12. JESUS UNDERSTOOD TIMING AND PREPARATION.

13. JESUS DEVELOPED A PASSION FOR HIS GOALS.

14. JESUS RESPECTED AUTHORITY.

15. JESUS NEVER DISCRIMINATED.

16. JESUS OFFERED INCENTIVES.

17. JESUS OVERCAME THE STIGMA OF A QUESTIONABLE BACKGROUND.

18. JESUS NEVER WASTED TIME ANSWERING CRITICS.

19. JESUS KNEW THERE WAS A RIGHT TIME AND A WRONG TIME TO APPROACH PEOPLE.

20. JESUS EDUCATED HIS DOWN-LINE.

21. JESUS REFUSED TO BE DISCOURAGED WHEN OTHERS MISJUDGED HIS MOTIVES.

22. JESUS REFUSED TO BE BITTER WHEN OTHERS WERE DISLOYAL OR BETRAYED HIM.

23. JESUS NETWORKED WITH PEOPLE OF ALL BACKGROUNDS.

24. JESUS RESISTED TEMPTATION.

25. JESUS MADE DECISIONS THAT CREATED A DESIRED FUTURE INSTEAD OF A DESIRED PRESENT.

26. JESUS NEVER JUDGED PEOPLE BY THEIR OUTWARD APPEARANCE.

27. JESUS RECOGNIZED THE LAW OF REPETITION.

28. JESUS WAS A TOMORROW-THINKER.

29. JESUS KNEW THAT MONEY ALONE COULD NOT BRING CONTENTMENT.

30. JESUS KNEW THE POWER OF WORDS AND THE POWER OF SILENCE.

31. JESUS KNEW WHEN YOU WANTED SOMETHING YOU HAVE NEVER HAD, YOU HAVE GOT TO DO SOMETHING YOU HAVE NEVER DONE.

32. JESUS PERMITTED OTHERS TO CORRECT THEIR MISTAKES.

33. JESUS KNEW HIS WORTH.

34. JESUS NEVER TRIED TO SUCCEED ALONE.

35. JESUS KNEW THAT MONEY IS ANYWHERE YOU REALLY WANT IT TO BE.

36. JESUS SET SPECIFIC GOALS.

37. JESUS KNEW THAT EVERY GREAT ACHIEVEMENT REQUIRED A WILLINGNESS TO BEGIN SMALL.

38. JESUS HURT WHEN OTHERS HURT.

39. JESUS WAS NOT AFRAID TO SHOW HIS FEELINGS.

40. JESUS KNEW THE POWER OF HABIT.

41. JESUS FINISHED WHAT HE STARTED.

42. JESUS WAS KNOWLEDGEABLE OF SCRIPTURE.

43. JESUS NEVER HURRIED.

44. JESUS WENT WHERE HE WAS CELEBRATED.

45. JESUS CONSISTENTLY CONSULTED HIS UP-LINE.

46. JESUS KNEW THAT PRAYER GENERATED RESULTS.

47. JESUS ROSE EARLY.

48. JESUS NEVER FELT HE HAD TO PROVE HIMSELF TO ANYONE.

49. JESUS AVOIDED UNNECESSARY CONFRONTATIONS.

50. JESUS DELEGATED.

51. JESUS CAREFULLY GUARDED HIS PERSONAL SCHEDULE.

52. JESUS ASKED QUESTIONS TO ACCURATELY DETERMINE THE NEEDS AND DESIRES OF OTHERS.

53. JESUS ALWAYS ANSWERED TRUTHFULLY.

54. JESUS STAYED IN THE CENTER OF HIS EXPERTISE.

55. JESUS ACCEPTED THE RESPONSIBILITY FOR THE MISTAKES OF HIS DOWN-LINE.

56. JESUS PURSUED THE MENTORSHIP OF MORE EXPERIENCED MEN.

57. JESUS DID NOT PERMIT HIS DOWN-LINE TO SHOW DISRESPECT.

58. JESUS UNDERSTOOD SEED-FAITH.

WISDOM PRINCIPLES

1. A PRODUCTIVE LIFE IS NOT AN ACCIDENT.

2. NEVER SPEAK WORDS THAT MAKE SATAN THINK HE'S WINNING.

3. ADVERSITY IS BREEDING GROUND FOR MIRACLES.

4. THOSE WHO ARE UNWILLING TO LOSE, RARELY DO.

5. LIFE CHANGES ONLY WHEN YOUR DAILY PRIORITIES CHANGE.

6. HAPPINESS IS MOVEMENT TOWARD THAT WHICH IS RIGHT.

7. NO ONE HAS BEEN A LOSER LONGER THAN SATAN.

8. THOSE WHO DO NOT RESPECT YOUR TIME WILL NOT RESPECT YOUR WISDOM EITHER.

9. STOP LOOKING AT WHAT YOU SEE AND START LOOKING AT WHAT YOU CAN HAVE.

10. INTOLERANCE OF THE PRESENT CREATES A FUTURE.

11. FORGIVENESS IS NOT A SUGGESTION, BUT A REQUIREMENT.

12. WHOEVER CANNOT INCREASE YOU, WILL EVENTUALLY DECREASE YOU.

13. TODAY IS THE TOMORROW YOU TALKED ABOUT YESTERDAY.

14. YOUR WORDS ARE SIGNPOSTS TO OTHERS... POINTING IN THE DIRECTION YOUR LIFE IS MOVING.

15. YOU WILL NEVER REACH YOUR POTENTIAL UNTIL YOUR PRIORITIES BECOME HABITUAL.

16. YOUR LIFE CALLING IS USUALLY WHATEVER CREATES THE HIGHEST LEVEL OF JOY WITHIN YOU.

17. YOU WILL NEVER POSSESS WHAT YOU ARE UNWILLING TO PURSUE.

18. YOUR PAIN CAN BECOME YOUR PASSAGE TO THE GREATEST MIRACLE OF YOUR LIFE.

19. YOU WILL NEVER REACH THE PALACE TALKING LIKE A PEASANT.

20. STOP LOOKING AT WHERE YOU HAVE BEEN AND START LOOKING AT WHERE YOU CAN BE.

21. YOUR WORDS ARE DECIDING YOUR FUTURE.

22. A TRUE WINNER WILL NEVER MAGNIFY HIS PERSONAL WEAKNESS.

23. YOU CAN ONLY MOVE AWAY FROM A BAD THOUGHT BY DELIBERATELY MOVING TOWARD A GOOD ONE.

24. CHAMPIONS...SIMPLY MAKE AN EXTRA ATTEMPT.

25. YOUR CONTRIBUTION TO OTHERS DETERMINES GOD'S CONTRIBUTION TO YOU.

26. ANY DISORDER IN YOUR LIFE CAN CREATE THE DEATH OF YOUR DREAM.

27. THE PROOF OF DESIRE IS PURSUIT.

28. WHATEVER YOU THINK ABOUT MOST IS REALLY YOUR GOD.

29. PROSPERITY IS SIMPLY HAVING ENOUGH OF GOD'S PROVISIONS TO COMPLETE HIS INSTRUCTIONS FOR YOUR LIFE.

30. SELFISHNESS IS DEPRIVING ANOTHER TO BENEFIT YOURSELF.

31. GIVING IS PROOF THAT YOU HAVE CONQUERED GREED.

32. WHEN YOU LET GO OF WHAT IS IN YOUR HAND, GOD WILL LET GO OF WHAT IS IN HIS HAND FOR YOU.

33. WHEN WHAT YOU HOLD IN YOUR HAND IS NOT ENOUGH TO BE A HARVEST, MAKE IT A SEED.

34. YOUR SEED IS LIKE A PURCHASE ORDER IN THE WAREHOUSE OF HEAVEN... AUTHORIZING MIRACLE PACKAGES TO BE SENT INTO YOUR LIFE.

35. SATAN'S FAVORITE ENTRY INTO YOUR LIFE IS USUALLY THROUGH THOSE CLOSEST TO YOU.

36. CONFIDENTIALITY IS ONE OF THE MOST TREASURED GIFTS YOU CAN GIVE TO ANOTHER.

37. STOP LOOKING AT WHERE YOU HAVE BEEN AND BEGIN LOOKING AT WHERE YOU ARE GOING.

38. WHAT YOUR MIND CANNOT MASTER, IT WILL EVENTUALLY RESENT.

39. ANGER WILL NEVER CREATE PERMANENT COOPERATION FROM ANOTHER.

40. THE BROKEN BECOME MASTERS AT MENDING.

41. DON'T POISON YOUR FUTURE WITH THE PAIN OF THE PAST.

42. WHAT YOU FAIL TO DESTROY, WILL EVENTUALLY DESTROY YOU.

43. DEPRESSION WILL ALWAYS FOLLOW ANY DECISION TO AVOID A PRIORITY.

44. WHEN FATIGUE WALKS IN, FAITH WALKS OUT.

45. LONELINESS IS NOT A LOSS OF AFFECTION BUT THE LOSS OF DIRECTION.

46. IMMATURITY IS THE INABILITY TO DELAY SELF-GRATIFICATION.

47. YOUR SELF-WORTH IS NOT DETERMINED BY YOUR PAST MISTAKES, BUT BY YOUR WILLINGNESS TO RECOGNIZE THEM.

48. REPENTANCE IS ALWAYS THE FIRST STEP TO RECOVERY.

49. FAILURE WILL LAST ONLY AS LONG AS YOU PERMIT IT.

50. MEN DO NOT REALLY DECIDE THEIR FUTURE... THEY DECIDE THEIR HABITS—THEN, THEIR HABITS DECIDE THEIR FUTURE.

51. YESTERDAY'S FAILURE...CAN BECOME THE CATALYST FOR TOMORROW'S SUCCESS.

52. IF GOD CUSHIONED EVERY BLOW, YOU WOULD NEVER LEARN TO GROW.

53. CONFESSION IS A FAITH-RELEASER INTO TOTAL RESTORATION.

54. YOUR CONTRIBUTION TO OTHERS DETERMINES WHAT GOD WILL CONTRIBUTE TO YOU.

55. YOUR LIFE WILL ALWAYS MOVE IN THE DIRECTION OF YOUR STRONGEST THOUGHT.

56. YOU ARE NEVER AS FAR FROM A MIRACLE AS IT FIRST APPEARS.

57. YOU'LL NEVER LEAVE WHERE YOU ARE UNTIL YOU DECIDE WHERE YOU'D RATHER BE.

58. WHEN YOU GET INTO THE WORD —THE WORD WILL GET INTO YOU.

59. PAIN IS OFTEN A BRIDGE, NOT A BARRICADE TO SUCCESS.

60. YOU CREATE A SEASON OF SUCCESS EVERY TIME YOU COMPLETE AN INSTRUCTION FROM GOD.

61. YOU WILL ALWAYS STRUGGLE, SUBCONSCIOUSLY TO BECOME THE SELF-PORTRAIT YOU BELIEVE YOURSELF TO BE.

62. THE DAY YOU MAKE A DECISION ABOUT YOUR LIFE IS THE DAY YOUR WORLD WILL CHANGE.

63. YOUR HARVEST WILL ALWAYS COME THROUGH THE DOOR OF SOMEONE IN TROUBLE, WHO IS NEEDING YOUR HELP.

64. THE SEASON OF YOUR LIFE WILL CHANGE EVERY TIME YOU DECIDE TO USE YOUR FAITH.

65. NEVER STAY WHERE GOD HAS NOT ASSIGNED YOU.

66. TOMORROW CONTAINS MORE JOY THAN ANY YESTERDAY YOU CAN RECALL.

DECISION

DR. MIKE MURDOCK

is in tremendous demand as one of the most dynamic speakers in America today.

Will You Accept Jesus As Your Personal Savior Today?

The Bible says, "That if thou shalt confess with thy mouth the Lord Jesus, and shalt believe in thine heart that God hath raised Him from the dead, thou shalt be saved" (Rom. 10:9).

Pray this prayer from your heart today!

"Dear Jesus, I believe that You died for me and rose again on the third day. I confess I am a sinner...I need Your love and forgiveness... Come into my heart. Forgive my sins. I receive your eternal life. Confirm Your love by giving me peace, joy and supernatural love for others. Amen."

More than 14,000 audiences in 38 countries have attended his meetings and seminars. Hundreds of invitations come to him from churches, colleges and business corporations. He is a noted author of over 130 books, including the best sellers, *"The Leadership Secrets of Jesus"* and *"Secrets of the Richest Man Who Ever Lived."* Thousands view his weekly television program, *"Wisdom Keys with Mike Murdock."* Many attend his Saturday School of Wisdom Breakfasts that he hosts in major cities of America.

Clip and Mail

☐ Yes, Mike! I made a decision to accept Christ as my personal Savior today. Please send me my free gift of your book, *"31 Keys to a New Beginning"* to help me with my new life in Christ. *(B-48)*

NAME _____ BIRTHDAY _____

ADDRESS _____

CITY _____ STATE ____ ZIP _____

PHONE _____ E-MAIL _____ *B-72*

Mail form to:
The Wisdom Center • *P. O. Box 99* •*Denton, TX 76202*
Phone: 1-888-WISDOM-1 (1-888-947-3661)
*Website: **www.thewisdomcenter.cc***

DR. MIKE MURDOCK

1 Has embraced his Assignment to Pursue...Proclaim...and Publish the Wisdom of God to help people achieve their dreams and goals.

2 Began full-time evangelism at the age of 19, which has continued since 1966.

3 Has traveled and spoken to more than 14,000 audiences in 38 countries, including East and West Africa, the Orient, and Europe.

4 Noted author of 130 books, including best sellers, "Wisdom For Winning," "Dream Seeds" and "The Double Diamond Principle."

5 Created the popular "Topical Bible" series for Businessmen, Mothers, Fathers, Teenagers; "The One-Minute Pocket Bible" series, and "The Uncommon Life" series.

6 Has composed more than 5,700 songs such as "I Am Blessed," "You Can Make It," "God Rides On Wings Of Love" and "Jesus Just The Mention Of Your Name," recorded by many gospel artists.

7 Is the Founder of The Wisdom Center, in Denton, Texas.

8 Has a weekly television program called "Wisdom Keys With Mike Murdock."

9 Has appeared often on TBN, CBN and other television network programs.

10 Is a Founding Trustee on the Board of International Charismatic Bible Ministries with Oral Roberts.

11 Has had more than 3,500 accept the call into full-time ministry under his ministry.

THE MINISTRY

1 **Wisdom Books & Literature** - Over 130 best-selling Wisdom Books and 70 Teaching Tape Series.

2 **Church Crusades** - Multitudes are ministered to in crusades and seminars throughout America in "The Uncommon Wisdom Conferences." Known as a man who loves pastors, he has focused on church crusades for 36 years.

3 **Music Ministry** - Millions have been blessed by the anointed songwriting and singing of Mike Murdock, who has made over 15 music albums and CDs available.

4 **Television** - "Wisdom Keys With Mike Murdock," a nationally-syndicated weekly television program.

5 **The Wisdom Center** - The Ministry Offices where Dr. Murdock holds an annual School of Wisdom for those desiring The Uncommon Life.

6 **Schools of the Holy Spirit** - Mike Murdock hosts Schools of the Holy Spirit in many churches to mentor believers on the Person and Companionship of the Holy Spirit.

7 **Schools of Wisdom** - In 24 major cities Mike Murdock hosts Saturday Schools of Wisdom for those who want personalized and advanced training for achieving "The Uncommon Dream."

8 **Missionary Ministry** - Dr. Murdock's overseas outreaches to 38 countries have included crusades in East and West Africa, South America and Europe.

Will You Become A Wisdom Key Partner?

The Assignment Of This Ministry Is To Pursue, Proclaim And Publish The Wisdom Of God.

1. **Television & Radio** - *"Wisdom Keys With Mike Murdock,"* a nationally-syndicated weekly television program features Mike Murdock's teaching and music.

2. **The Wisdom Center** - The Ministry offices where Dr. Murdock holds an annual School of Wisdom for those desiring The Uncommon Life.

3. **Missionary Ministry** - Dr. Murdock's overseas outreaches to 38 countries have included crusades in East and West Africa, South America and Europe.

4. **Music Ministry** - Millions of people have been blessed by the anointed songwriting and singing of Mike Murdock, who has made over 15 music albums and CDs available.

5. **Wisdom Books & Literature** - Over 120 best-selling Wisdom Books and 70 Teaching Tape Series.

6. **Church Crusades** - Multitudes are ministered to in crusades and seminars throughout America in "The Uncmmon Wisdom Conference." Known as a man who loves pastors has focused on church crusades for 36 years.

7. **Schools of Wisdom** - In 24 major cities Mike Murdock hosts Saturday Schools of Wisdom for those who want personalized and advanced training for achieving "The Uncommon Life."

8. **Schools of the Holy Spirit** - Mike Murdock hosts Schools of the Holy Spirit in many churches to mentor believers on the Person and Companionship of the Holy Spirit.

I want to personally invite you to be a part of this ministry!

WISDOM KEY PARTNERSHIP PLAN

Dear Partner,
God has connected us.
Will you become a Wisdom Key Faith Partner with my ministry? Your monthly Seeds are so powerful in helping heal broken lives. When you sow into the work of God, four Miracle Harvests are guaranteed in Scripture:

▶ Uncommon Protection (Mal. 3:10,11)
▶ Uncommon Favor (Lk. 6:38)
▶ Uncommon Health (Isa. 58:8)
▶ Uncommon Financial Ideas and Wisdom
   (Deut. 8:18)

Your Faith Partner,

Mike Murdock

❏ Yes, Mike, I want to be a Wisdom Key Partner with you. Please rush The Wisdom Key Partnership Pak to me today!

❏ **Y**es, Mike, I want to be a Wisdom Key Monthly Partner. Enclosed is my first monthly Seed-Faith Promise of $_____.   Total Enclosed $ _____

Name _____ Birthdate ____/____

Address _____

City _____ State _____ Zip _____

Phone (_____) _____ E-Mail _____

B-72

Clip and Mail

WISDOM KEY BOOKS

Cat. #	No. Ea.	Wisdom Key Books $3.00 each book	Total Price
B02		Five Steps Out Of Depression	
B03		The Sex Trap	
B04		Ten Lies Many People Believe About Money	
B05		Finding Your Purpose In Life	
B06		Creating Tomorrow Through Seed-Faith	
B07		Battle Techniques For War Weary Saints	
B08		Enjoying the Winning Life	
B09		Four Forces That Guarantee Career Success	
B10		The Bridge Called Divorce	
B55		20 Keys To A Happier Marriage	
B56		How To Turn Mistakes Into Miracles	
B64		Seven Obstacles To Abundant Success	
B65		Born To Taste The Grapes	
B66		Greed, Gold and Giving	
B69		Wisdom Keys For A Powerful Prayer Life	
B80		The Greatest Success Habit On Earth	
		Total Items Ordered Sub Total	
		Add 10% Shipping	
		Total Enclosed	

Name _____

Address _____

City _____ State _____ Zip _____

☐ Visa   ☐ AMEX   ☐ MC   Expiration Date _____

☐ Discover   ☐ Money Order   ☐ Cash   ☐ Check

Card # _____

Authorized Signature _____

Mail To:
The Wisdom Center · *P.O. Box 99 · Denton, TX 76202*
1-888-WISDOM-1 (1-888-947-3661)
Website: ***www.thewisdomcenter.cc***

ORDER FORM THE WISDOM CENTER
(All books paperback unless indicated otherwise.)

Qty	Code	Book Title	USA	Total
	B-01	Wisdom For Winning	$10	
	B-02	Five Steps Out Of Depression	$ 3	
	B-03	The Sex Trap	$ 3	
	B-04	Ten Lies People Believe About Money	$ 3	
	B-05	Finding Your Purpose In Life	$ 3	
	B-06	Creating Tomorrow Through Seed-Faith	$ 3	
	B-07	Battle Techniques For War Weary Saints	$ 3	
	B-08	Enjoying The Winning Life	$ 3	
	B-09	Four Forces/Guarantee Career Success	$ 3	
	B-10	The Bridge Called Divorce	$ 3	
	B-11	Dream Seeds	$ 9	
	B-12	The Ministers Encyclopedia, Vol. 1	$20	
	B-13	Seeds Of Wisdom On Dreams And Goals, Vol. 1	$ 3	
	B-14	Seeds Of Wisdom On Relationships, Vol. 2	$ 3	
	B-15	Seeds Of Wisdom On Miracles, Vol. 3	$ 3	
	B-16	Seeds Of Wisdom On Seed-Faith, Vol. 4	$ 3	
	B-17	Seeds Of Wisdom On Overcoming, Vol. 5	$ 3	
	B-18	Seeds Of Wisdom On Habits, Vol. 6	$ 3	
	B-19	Seeds Of Wisdom On Warfare, Vol. 7	$ 3	
	B-20	Seeds Of Wisdom On Obedience, Vol. 8	$ 3	
	B-21	Seeds Of Wisdom On Adversity, Vol. 9	$ 3	
	B-22	Seeds Of Wisdom On Prosperity, Vol. 10	$ 3	
	B-23	Seeds Of Wisdom On Prayer, Vol. 11	$ 3	
	B-24	Seeds Of Wisdom On Faith-Talk, Vol. 12	$ 3	
	B-25	7 Kinds Of People You Cannot Help	$ 5	
	B-26	The God Book	$10	
	B-27	The Jesus Book	$10	
	B-28	The Blessing Bible	$10	
	B-29	The Survival Bible	$10	
	B-30	The Teens Topical Bible	$ 8	
	B-31	Seeds Of Wisdom Topical Bible	$15	
	B-32	The Minister's Topical Bible	$ 8	
	B-33	The Businessman's Topical Bible	$ 8	
	B-34	The Grandparent's Topical Bible	$ 8	
	B-35	The Father's Topical Bible	$ 8	
	B-36	The Mother's Topical Bible	$ 8	
	B-37	The New Believer's Topical Bible	$ 8	
	B-38	The Widow's Topical Bible	$ 8	
	B-39	The Double Diamond Principle	$ 9	
	B-40	Wisdom For Crisis Times	$ 9	
	B-41	The Gift Of Wisdom, Vol. 1	$10	
	B-42	One-Minute Businessman's Devotional	$12	
	B-43	One-Minute Businesswoman's Devotional	$12	
	B-44	31 Secrets For Career Success	$10	
	B-45	101 Wisdom Keys	$ 5	
	B-46	31 Facts About Wisdom	$ 5	
	B-47	The Covenant Of The Fifty-Eight Blessings	$ 8	
	B-48	31 Keys To A New Beginning	$ 5	
	B-49	The Proverbs 31 Woman	$ 7	
	B-50	One-Minute Pocket Bible For The Achiever	$ 5	
	B-51	One-Minute Pocket Bible For Fathers	$ 5	
	B-52	One-Minute Pocket Bible For Mothers	$ 5	
	B-53	One-Minute Pocket Bible For Teenagers	$ 5	
	B-54	The One-Minute Daily Devotional	$ 5	
	B-55	20 Keys To A Happier Marriage	$ 3	
	B-56	How To Turn Mistakes Into Miracles	$ 3	

Qty	Code	Book Title	USA	Total
	B-57	31 Secrets Of An Unforgettable Woman	$ 9	
	B-58	The Mentors Manna On Attitude	$ 3	
	B-59	The Making Of A Champion	$ 8	
	B-60	One-Minute Pocket Bible For Men	$ 5	
	B-61	One-Minute Pocket Bible For Women	$ 5	
	B-62	One-Minute Pocket Bible/Bus.Professionals	$ 5	
	B-63	One-Minute Pocket Bible For Truckers	$ 5	
	B-64	Seven Obstacles To Abundant Success	$ 3	
	B-65	Born To Taste The Grapes	$ 3	
	B-66	Greed, Gold And Giving	$ 3	
	B-67	Gift Of Wisdom For Champions	$10	
	B-68	Gift Of Wisdom For Achievers	$10	
	B-69	Wisdom Keys For A Powerful Prayer Life	$ 3	
	B-70	Gift Of Wisdom For Mothers	$10	
	B-71	Wisdom - God's Golden Key To Success	$ 7	
	B-72	The Double Diamond Daily Devotional	$15	
	B-73	The Mentors Manna On Abilities	$ 3	
	B-74	The Assignment: Dream/Destiny, Vol. 1	$10	
	B-75	The Assignment: Anointing/Adversity, Vol. 2	$10	
	B-76	The Mentors Manna On Assignment	$ 3	
	B-77	The Gift Of Wisdom For Fathers	$10	
	B-78	The Mentors Manna On The Secret Place	$ 3	
	B-79	The Mentors Manna On Achievement	$ 3	
	B-80	The Greatest Success Habit On Earth	$ 3	
	B-81	The Mentors Manna On Adversity	$ 3	
	B-82	31 Reasons People Do Not Receive Their Financial Harvest	$12	
	B-83	The Gift Of Wisdom For Wives	$10	
	B-84	The Gift Of Wisdom For Husbands	$10	
	B-85	The Gift Of Wisdom For Teenagers	$10	
	B-86	The Gift Of Wisdom For Leaders	$10	
	B-87	The Gift Of Wisdom For Graduates	$10	
	B-88	The Gift Of Wisdom For Brides	$10	
	B-89	The Gift Of Wisdom For Grooms	$10	
	B-90	The Gift Of Wisdom For Ministers	$10	
	B-91	The Leadership Secrets Of Jesus	$10	
	B-92	Secrets Of The Journey, Vol. 1	$ 5	
	B-93	Secrets Of The Journey, Vol. 2	$ 5	
	B-94	Secrets Of The Journey, Vol. 3	$ 5	
	B-95	Secrets Of The Journey, Vol. 4	$ 5	
	B-96	Secrets Of The Journey, Vol. 5	$ 5	
	B-97	The Assignment: Trials/Triumphs, Vol. 3	$ 5	
	B-98	The Assignment: Pain/Passion, Vol. 4	$ 5	
	B-99	Secrets Of The Richest Man Who Ever Lived	$10	
	B-100	The Holy Spirit Handbook, Vol. 1	$10	
	B-101	The 3 Most Important Things In Your Life	$10	
	B-102	Secrets Of The Journey, Vol. 6	$ 5	
	B-103	Secrets Of The Journey, Vol. 7	$ 5	
	B-104	7 Days To 1000 Times More	$10	
	B-105	31 Days To Succeeding On Your Job	$10	
	B-106	The Uncommon Leader	$ 5	
	B-107	The Uncommon Minister, Vol. 1	$ 5	
	B-108	The Uncommon Minister, Vol. 2	$ 5	
	B-109	The Uncommon Minister, Vol. 3	$ 5	
	B-110	The Uncommon Minister, Vol. 4	$ 5	
	B-111	The Uncommon Minister, Vol. 5	$ 5	
	B-112	The Uncommon Minister, Vol. 6	$ 5	
	B-113	The Uncommon Minister, Vol. 7	$ 5	

Qty	Code	Book Title	USA	Total
	B-114	The Law of Recognition	$10	
	B-115	Seeds of Wisdom on the Secret Place, Vol. 13	$ 5	
	B-116	Seeds of Wisdom on the Holy Spirit, Vol. 14	$ 5	
	B-117	Seeds of Wisdom on the Word Of God, Vol. 15	$ 5	
	B-118	Seeds of Wisdom on Problem Solving, Vol. 16	$ 5	
	B-119	Seeds of Wisdom on Favor, Vol. 17	$ 5	
	B-120	Seeds of Wisdom on Healing, Vol. 18	$ 5	
	B-121	Seeds of Wisdom on Time-Management, Vol. 19	$ 5	
	B-122	Seeds of Wisdom on Your Assignment, Vol. 20	$ 5	
	B-123	Seeds of Wisdom on Financial Breakthrough, Vol. 21	$ 5	
	B-124	Seeds of Wisdom on Enemies, Vol. 22	$ 5	
	B-125	Seeds of Wisdom on Decision-Making, Vol. 23	$ 5	
	B-126	Seeds of Wisdom on Mentorship Vol. 24	$ 5	
	B-127	Seeds of Wisdom on Goal-Setting, Vol. 25	$ 5	
	B-128	Seeds of Wisdom on the Power of Words, Vol. 26	$ 5	
	B-129	The Secret of the Seed	$10	
	B-130	The Uncommon Millionaire, Vol. 1	$10	
	B-131	The Uncommon Father	$ 8	
	B-132	The Uncommon Mother	$ 8	
	B-133	The Uncommon Achiever	$10	
	B-134	The Uncommon Armorbearer	$10	
	B-135	The Uncommon Dream, Vol. 1	$10	
	B-136	The Wisdom Commentary, Vol 1 (Seed-gift)	$100	

☐ CASH ☐ CHECK ☐ MONEY ORDER ☐ VISA

CREDIT CARD # ☐ MC ☐ DISCOVER ☐ AMEX

EXPIRATION DATE [ ] [ ] [ ] [ ] *SORRY NO C.O.D.'s*

Signature _____

TOTAL PAGES 1, 2, 3	$
SHIPPING ADD 10%-USA/20%-OTHERS	$
CANADA CURRENCY DIFFERENCE ADD 20%	$
TOTAL ENCLOSED	$

PLEASE PRINT

Name _____

Address _____

City _____ State _____ Zip _____

Phone (____) ____ - _____

E-mail _____

Mail to: **The Wisdom Center** • P.O. Box 99 • Denton, TX 76202
1-888-WISDOM-1 (1-888-947-3661) • Website: **thewisdomcenter.cc**